The Cloud upon the Sanctuary

The *Cloud* upon
the *Sanctuary*

KARL VON ECKARTSHAUSEN

Absque nube pro nobis

TRANSLATED AND ANNOTATED BY
ISABELLE DE STEIGER
FOREWORD BY EDWARD DUNNING
PREFACE BY J. W. BRODIE-INNES
INTRODUCTION BY ARTHUR EDWARD WAITE

IBIS PRESS
AN IMPRINT OF NICOLAS-HAYS, INC.
BERWICK, MAINE

Published in 2003 by
Ibis Press
An Imprint of Nicolas-Hays, Inc.
P. O. Box 1126
Berwick, ME 03901-1126
www.nicolashays.com

Distributed by Red Wheel/Weiser LLC
Box 612
York Beach, ME 03901-0612
www.redwheelweiser.com

Cataloging-in-Publication Data is available by request
at the Library of Congress

Cover design by Phillip Augusta.
Cover photograph copyright © 2003 Phillip Augusta.
Typeset in Garamond and Old Style 7 9/11
Printed in the United States of America

VG

09 08 07 06 05 04 03
8 7 6 5 4 3 2 1

CONTENTS

FOREWORD

IN MARCH 1909, with much sound and fury but with little effect on the reading public, Aleister Crowley published the first issue of *The Equinox*. As befitted "The Official Organ of the A∴A∴" it included "An Account of A∴A∴," written by Crowley himself—except for the material he had borrowed from Isabelle de Steiger's English translation of *The Cloud upon the Sanctuary*. Eckartshausen's work is, ostensibly, openly and avowedly Christian in both tone and content, so why did Crowley—than whom anyone less Christian can scarcely be imagined—make use of it?

As with many of Crowley's borrowings, the answer is that it served his purpose at the time. The Argenteum Astrum, Crowley's variant and extension of the Hermetic Order of the Golden Dawn, had been officially founded in November 1907. Its most obvious difference from its involuntary parent is the inclusion of Third Order grades above that of Adeptus Exemptus, and it is not surprising that the implicit possibility of such perilous but ecstatic attainment would attract to the A∴A∴ potential members of a decidedly elitist temperament. To such magicians, Eckartsausen's concept of an Interior Church, a hidden assembly composed of elect souls only, would appeal mightily. Given that *The Equinox* was a secondary source for the concept, aspiring Magi can be forgiven for misunderstanding Eckartshausen; Crowley, who had read the English translation, cannot—he was guilty of a deliberate misreading of the text.

Early in 1898, while he was still at Cambridge, Crowley had purchased a copy of A. E. Waite's *The Book of Black Magic* and, intrigued by a tantalizing suggestion in the text, wrote to him. According to Crowley the passage in question "hinted that [Waite] knew of a Hidden Church withdrawn from the world in whose sanctuaries were preserved the true mysteries of initiation."[1] In fact, Waite made no reference to a "Hidden Church" and did not suggest that he knew how it might be entered. The two passages that inspired Crowley to write Waite, and which he inaccurately conflated thirty years later, are these:

> It would be unbecoming in a professed transcendentalist to deny that there is a Magic which is behind Magic, or that the occult sanctuaries possess their secrets and mysteries.[2]
>
> All students of occultism are perfectly well aware of the existence in modern times of more than one Mystical Fraternity, deriving, or believed to derive, from other associations of the past. There are, of course, many unaffiliated occultists, but the secret Fraternities exist, and the keys of mystic symbolism are said to be in their possession.[3]

By 1898, Waite had resumed his membership of the Golden Dawn but had not entered the Second Order. He had no intention of inviting this unknown, "unaffiliated occultist" to join the Order, and suggested instead that Crowley might profit from reading *The Cloud upon the Sanctuary*. Crowley took Waite's advice and "with this book I retired to Wastdale Head for the Easter vacation of 1898."[4] He was impressed with Eckartshausen's ideas and, as a result of coincidental meetings with two existing members, Julian Baker and George Cecil Jones, he was able to enter the Golden Dawn in the expectation of finding within it that "invisible and interior Church" of which Eckartshausen had written. In this pious hope he was disappointed, but he valued the essential features of *The Cloud upon the Sanctuary* and eventually made use of them in propagating the Argenteum Astrum. And despite his constant public sniping at both the man and his work, he admitted—

[1] John Symonds and Kenneth Grant, eds., *The Confessions of Aleister Crowley. An Autohagiography* (London: Cape, 1969), p. 127.

[2] A. E. Waite, *The Book of Black Magic and of Pacts*, 1898 ed. (Reprinted as *The Book of Black Magic* [York Beach, ME: Weiser, 1972]), p. vii.

[3] Waite, *Book of Black Magic*, p. 11.

[4] Symonds and Grant, *Confessions of Aleister Crowley*, p. 127.

privately and many years later—his debt to Waite: "If it had not been for Waite, I doubt if, humanly speaking, I should ever have got in touch with the Great Order."[5]

We do not know the exact words in which Crowley addressed his questions to Waite, but they presumably indicated that the writer was an aspiring magician in search of a magical order. Waite, however, was never happy with ritual magic—he looked upon the "written ceremonial" of the "secret Fraternities" as "either a debased and scandalous travesty or a trivial and misconstrued application"[6]—and for him, the Golden Dawn was an esoteric rather than a magical order, offering a viable path toward spiritual regeneration. From this point of view, *The Cloud upon the Sanctuary* was an ideal text for guiding a young aspirant to initiation away from the pitfalls of practical magic.

What is not clear is precisely how Waite interpreted Eckartshausen in 1898, but he evidently looked upon him as something other than an orthodox Christian mystic and felt that his work was appropriate for members of the Golden Dawn. Others certainly shared such a view, and Mme. de Steiger's translation of *The Cloud upon the Sanctuary* can be seen, in a sense, as a product of the Order. It was first published in 1895 in *The Unknown World*, a magazine edited by Waite and devoted to "The Occult Sciences, Magic, Mystical Philosophy, Alchemy," and other similar subjects. From the first issue of the magazine, it had been Waite's intention to undertake "the translation or reproduction of rare or important occult works," and when he chose Eckartshausen's work to begin this project, it was because "we have been guided by its close correspondence with certain aspects of Christian mystical opinion at the present day."[7]

In the same editorial, Waite went on to write that, "A revered Kabalist, the 'disciple and literary heir' of an illustrious French transcendentalist," had written to one of the magazine's regular contributors, to say that,

---

[5] Letter to Louis Wilkinson, 30 December 1944. In the Aleister Crowley Collection, Harry Ransom Humanities Research Center, University of Texas at Austin.

[6] Waite, *Book of Black Magic*, p. vii.

[7] *The Unknown World* 1, no. 6 (15 January, 1895): 241.

> I hear with pleasure that *The Unknown
> World* will give a translation of *The Cloud
> upon the Sanctuary*. This little book, which
> bears for epigraph—*sine nube pro nobis*—is
> admirable for its insight and suggestiveness.
> One would say that it is written recently. It
> is the best mystic work for our time.[8]

The Kabalist was not named, but the description most closely
fits Dr. Westcott.

Within a year, the translation had been published in book
form, with an enthusiastic preface by J. W. Brodie-Innes. Both
he and Mme. de Steiger were active members of the Golden
Dawn, as was the newly re-admitted Waite, while Westcott's
endorsement cemented the connection between the translated
text and the Order in which it circulated (the Golden Dawn
library held the translation in both book *and* magazine form).[9]
But was Eckartshausen's "last Swan's Song," as Mme. de
Steiger described it, truly a text designed, or at least suitable for
Western esotericists?

She certainly thought that it was, and her notes on the
text are designed to present it as an esoteric interpretation of
Christian doctrine, based upon Eckartshausen's experimental
knowledge of the regenerative process as it operates on the
human spirit.

Necessarily, she felt *The Cloud upon the Sanctuary* was
"understood thoroughly only by minds in [Eckartshausen's]
own grade of office" and that it was "to such he still speaks
principally."[10] In other words, it is a text for a spiritual elite, not
for "the multitude [who] are not prone to philosophy, they need
children's food" (p. 128 *infra*). It is also true that some aspects
of Eckartshausen's life, and the nature of some of his works,
could lead the uncritical observer to conclude that *The Cloud
upon the Sanctuary* was designed for a circle of adepts who
alone would be able to attain entrance to the exalted spiritual
company about which he writes.

Eckartshausen was an enthusiastic student of both alchemy
and numerology, his published works include historical and

---

[8] *The Unknown World* 1, no. 6 (15 January, 1895): 241.

[9] In the catalogue of the "Second Order Library" No. 178 is *The Unknown World*,
and No. 455 is *The Cloud upon the Sanctuary*.

[10] *The Unknown World* 2 (1895): 208.

philosophical studies of magic and alchemy, and he seems
to have been deeply interested in other branches of hermetic
symbolism.[11] As a young man, he had been a member of
Weishaupt's Order of the Illuminati, and his works were
widely read within the esoteric community in Europe, notably
by Louis Claude de Saint-Martin, I. V. Lopukhin, and Tsar
Alexander I. But these bald statements, true though they are,
require certain caveats.

His studies of alchemy led Eckartshausen to compose two
"Prayers for Alchemists":

> Light Supreme, who art the Divine in
> Nature and dwellest in its innermost parts
> as in Heaven, hallowed be thy qualities and
> laws!
>
> Wherever thou art, all is brought to
> perfection; may the realm of thy Knowledge
> become subject unto thee.
>
> May our will in all our work be only thee,
> self-moving Power of Light! And as in the
> whole of Nature thou accomplishest all
> things, so accomplish all things in our work
> also.
>
> Give us of the Dew of Heaven, and the Fat
> of the Earth, the Fruits of Sun and Moon
> from the Tree of Life.
>
> And forgive us all errors which we have
> committed in our work without knowledge
> of thee, as we seek to turn from their errors
> those who have offended our precepts. And
> leave us not to our own darkness and our
> own science, but deliver us from all evil
> through the perfection of thy Work, Amen.

---

[11] An unpublished manuscript translation of a work attributed to Eckartshausen,
Instruction de Cloas, prêtre de la Nature à Sophron (c. 1800), is described in the
Catalogue de la Libraririe Dorbon-Ainé (1929). It includes Egyptian, astrological,
and Rosicrucian symbols.

The second prayer is shorter:

> Hail, pure self-moving Source, O Form,
> pure for receiving the Light! The Light of
> all things unites itself with thee alone.
>
> Most blessed art thou among all receptive
> forms, and blessed is the Fruit that thou
> conceivest, the Essence of Light united
> with warm substance.
>
> Pure Form, Mother of the most perfect
> Being, lift thyself up to the Light for us,
> now as we toil and in the hour when we
> complete the Work![12]

Both of these prayers utilize the language, and incorporate familiar words and phrases from prayers in the Roman liturgy, which are themselves based on scriptural texts. The alchemical symbolism is used to express the relationship between God and His creation, and the prayers provide a perfect illustration of Eckartshausen's understanding of alchemy as a spiritual pursuit that aids the practitioner in the quest to enter the presence of God.

He looked upon numerology in the same light and meditated on numbers in order to learn their spiritual significance. That this was not simply an intellectual process is clear from a letter of Baron Kirchberger to Saint-Martin, in which he quotes Eckartshausen's account of the process by which he learned the attributes of the numbers 1 to 10. It is not by use of the intellect, but through the love of God:

> I possess no words in our language to explain
> how this happens; for the secrets of the world
> of spirits cannot be conceived by the under-
> standing unless they be seen also. . . . All that
> I can do is to impart to you the instruction
> which I myself have received. . . . I feel a
> higher presence. I am permitted to ask, and
> I receive answers and visions. The following
> are the steps by which, through the Lord's
> grace, I have advanced:

---

[12] From *Über die Zauberkräfte der Natur*. Munich, 1819. Translation courtesy of Joscelyn Godwin (Alchemy Web Site http//www.levity.com/alchemy/eckarts.html).

1. The Unity
2. The three powers therein.
3. The outspoken Word
4. The name of God in four letters.
5. The three-fold power in the four-fold, or 3+4 = 7
6. The active and intelligent Cause.
7. The holy name of this Cause.
8. How to pronounce this name.
9. The two tables of the law.
10. The law in full.[13]

Although the manipulation of numbers has a theurgic overtone, this is not present in Eckartshausen's process, which begins and ends with divine grace, and not with the will of the individual. The prayer that accompanies the letter makes this even more clear:

> Eternal Light! which shineth in the darkness, but which the darkness hath not comprehended! Who came to his own, and was not received by his own! To Thee, most Holy Light, I open my heart for a temple! Cleanse my heart and make it a temple for Thyself: from this day be my own will denied, and may Thy will become my holy rule; this Thy will be done on earth as in heaven; Light of Spirits, be my lamp; through Thee, Holy Word, may the Deity speak in me! Take me again into Thyself, who have lived separated from Thee. By Thy spirit quicken the dead letter in me, and, according to Thy promise, give to me power to become a child of God, *born to Thee*. Let Thy Word become flesh in me, and dwell in me, that I may see Thy glory, the glory as of the only begotten Son, full of grace and truth. Amen.[14]

---

[13] *Mystical Philosophy and Spirit-Manifestations. Selections from the recently published Correspondence between Louyis-Claude de Saint-Martin, and Kirchberger, Baron de Liebistorf, during the years 1792-97.* Translated and edited by Edwin Burton Penny. Exeter, 1863, pp. 209-210.

[14] *Mystical Philosophy*, p. 211.

Above all things, he is seeking to surrender his own will to that of God and to be regenerated, so that he may attain the presence of God. There is not the slightest hint of elitism, or of a desire for self-aggrandizement, nor any trace of the spiritual pride that bedevils magicians.

This should not surprise us, for Karl von Eckartshausen was, as Waite makes clear in his introduction to this translation, a pious and devout Roman Catholic. He had soon left the Illuminati and became bitterly, and very publicly, hostile to the Order. His most popular, and most frequently reprinted work was *God is Purest Love,*[15] a collection of wholly orthodox prayers, meditations, and devotional exercises. It should also be noted that *The Cloud upon the Sanctuary* was published openly, which would not have been the case had it been intended for a closed circle of the spiritually superior. And Eckartshausen cannot be blamed for those of his readers who took up his work because they already believed themselves to be part of such a spiritual elite.

The few writers on mysticism who combine scholarship with a sympathy for mystical experience, and who take account of him, have recognized Eckartshausen's importance as an expositor of the doctrine of regeneration. In so doing, they have also rescued him from the misinterpretations of occultists who, they rightly point out, are ignorant of mystical theology. Thus Mrs. Herman, while praising Isabelle de Steiger's "able and characteristic annotations" to her translation of *The Cloud upon the Sanctuary*, castigates her (together with Schuré and Wilmshurst) for having

> but the slightest and most superficial know-
> ledge of the theology they so light-heartedly
> dismiss as external, not to say childish; and
> that—what is of more importance—the eso-
> teric wisdom which they propose to sub-
> stitute for it is neither particularly wise nor
> excessively esoteric.[16]

---

[15] In German, *Gott ist die reinste Liebe*. It was published in 1790 and a French translation, *Dieu est l'amour le plus pur*, appeared in the following year.

[16] E. Herman, *The Meaning and Value of Mysticism*, 2nd ed., 1916, p. 291. The author was an authority on Christian spirituality, and on Quietism in particular.

The danger in this is that,

> a Mysticism that would ground its theology
> upon nothing more substantial than its own
> unsifted guesses is in danger of being over-
> taken by moral and spiritual decrepitude
> and degeneracy.[17]

These are harsh words indeed, but they serve to indicate how wide is the gulf between the Christian orthodoxy that Eckartshausen espoused and the beliefs of his occultist admirers. It is not, however, an unbridgeable gulf and much of Waite's introduction is devoted to building such a bridge. That this was possible was acknowledged even by Mrs. Herman. While she stated that the doctrine of the Holy Assembly "may be construed in the sense of a vicious esotericism," she also noted that,

> The most popular expression of this difficult
> doctrine is found in Eckartshausen's well-
> known tractate, *The Cloud upon the Sanc-
> tuary*, while its deeper and more exhaustive
> unfolding is enshrined in a largely anon-
> ymous and not easily accessible literature,
> which has been brilliantly utilised in the
> profound and erudite investigations of Mr.
> A. E. Waite.[18]

This literature was also known to Mme. de Steiger, who made use of it in her own writings on spiritual regeneration.

The authors concerned, mostly of the Victorian era,[19] were "Theosophists" in the sense of being devotees of the works of Jacob Boehme, and included Mary Anne Atwood, the author of *A Suggestive Inquiry into the Hermetic Mystery* (1850) and the "M.A.A." who was the co-dedicatee of the 1896 edition of *The Cloud upon the Sanctuary* (Brodie-Innes was the other).

---

[17] Herman, *The Meaning and Value of Mysticism*, p. 292.

[18] Herman, *The Meaning and Value of Mysticism*, p. 357.

[19] The most important were Edward Burton Penny and his wife Anne (who wrote extensively on Boehme), and Christopher Walton, author of an immense and almost impenetrable study of the works of William Law. The only one to remain anonymous is the author of *Le Mystère de la Croix* (1732), to which Waite refers in his introduction. An English edition of the French text was published in 1859.

Mrs. Atwood's theories had a profound influence, not only on
Isabelle de Steiger, but also upon the entire group of Christian
esotericists who gathered round Anna Kingsford, and who
provided a focus for "Theosophists" of the Behmenist kind who
had become disenchanted with the neo-Buddhist theosophy
of H. P. Blavtasky. Isabelle de Steiger was, however, the only
one of them to become an avid devotee of Mrs. Atwood and to
appreciate in full the concept of regeneration presented in the
Suggestive Inquiry.

And for all their theological naiveté, these esotericists saw
themselves as mystics rather than occultists, and placed an em-
phasis upon their Christian faith. They truly sought the path of
regeneration and looked upon reintegration with God as their
ultimate goal. But what *is* the Interior Church, or Holy Assembly,
in which they and Eckartshausen so fervently believed? By
1909—when this edition of Mme. de Steiger's translation was
published—Waite had come to accept that Eckartshausen was,
indeed, a true Christian mystic, and in his own, inimitable style
he sets out the doctrine of the Interior Church in his introduction
to the text. The provision of an additional, and more succinct,
account may not, however, come amiss.

The process of regeneration in the individual is described by
Evelyn Underhill as

> the birth of something new or the coming
> forth of something which has slept—since
> both these phrases are but metaphors for
> another and more secret operation—the
> eye is opened on Eternity; the self, abruptly
> made aware of Reality, comes forth from the
> cave of illusion like a child from the womb
> and begins to live upon the supersensual
> plane. Then she feels in her inmost part
> a new presence, a new consciousness—it
> were hardly an exaggeration to say a new
> Person—weak, demanding nurture, clearly
> destined to pass through many phases of

> development before its maturity is reached;
> yet of so strange a nature, that in comparison
> with its environment she may well regard it
> as Divine.[20]

She goes on to quote Eckartshausen:

> This change, this upsetting, is called re-
> birth. *To be born* simply means to enter
> into a world in which the senses dominate,
> in which wisdom and love languish in the
> bonds of individuality. To be *re-born* means
> to return to a world where the spirit of
> wisdom and love governs and animal-man
> obeys [Letter VI, p. 77].

It is, in other words, the beginning of the gradual elimination
of original sin—a process which cannot be completed in this
world. And those who are regenerate realise that they are part
of a wider, Interior Church. This is not, as Waite points out
(p. xiv *infra*), a "corporate body existing merely within the
Church and controlling or leading it from a specific local centre
in concealment." Rather, it is "a withdrawn brotherhood in
whose hands the experimental knowledge of God has remained
and increased. It is the doctrine of the esoteric Church of the
Illuminated."[21] And because it has its role in the exterior
world, we can recognize others who are a part of it for, as
Eckartshausen says, "If it be necessary that true members
should meet together, they find and recognise each other with
perfect certainty" (Letter II, p. 28).

Such meetings do have a very real value, as Robertson
Nicoll notes:

> It is one of the chief alleviations of the sor-
> row of earthly disunion that we may ever
> and anon come to the surprised and joyous
> consciousness that the brother who is bear-
> ing another name and is fighting in another
> army is in reality one with us in the Mystical

---

[20] *Mysticism: A study in the nature and development of Man's spiritual Consciousness*, 12th ed., 1930 p. 123.

[21] Sir W. Robertson Nicoll, *The Garden of Nuts. Mystical Expositions with an Essay on Christian Mysticism*, 1905, p. 69.

> Holy Church. . . . Wherefore it is the wont of
> mystics to claim this fellowship, and to ex-
> act recognition "in all houses, temples and
> tarrying places of the Fraternity."[22]

We should also realize that this is not simply a fellowship
within the wider Church, but within the community of all those
who seek regeneration. The path of return to God is open to
everyone who can recognize that they are imperfect, that they
need to seek spiritual rebirth, and that they will travel more
joyously in the company of others: with whom they will, at
last, see the cloud draw away and have the Presence in the
Sanctuary revealed to them.

EDWARD DUNNING
London, July 2003

EDWARD DUNNING is a leading exponent of the Mystical School
of masonic research and an authority on European esoteric
movements of the Romantic Era, with an especial interest in
Sigmund Bacstrom and English alchemical manuscripts of this
period. For many years, he worked in the petroleum industry,
but is now retired and lives at Hampstead in north London,
continuing his research and exercising his "family" of black
labradors.

---

[22] Nicoll, *The Garden of Nuts*, pp. 74-75.

PREFACE TO THE FIRST ENGLISH EDITION

I HAVE GLADLY agreed, at the request of my friend Madame de Steiger, to say a few words of introduction to her admirable translation of Councillor Eckartshausen's *Cloud upon the Sanctuary*; feeling as I do that the appearance in an English dress of this work is one of the greatest boons that has been conferred on English occult students since the publication of *The Perfect Way*. It will probably be long before Eckartshausen's work is fully appreciated, yet it is not too much to say that every sentence of this little work deserves to be most carefully read and re-read, and studied over and over again, and even then gone back upon by the student who has the capacity, with clairvoyant, psychic, and spiritual analysis, in order that the great and valuable truths embodied therein may be completely realised and brought home to the mind.

There are two classes of minds which unfortunately divide between them the bulk of thinking humanity in our age and country, whose prejudices and fixed ideals must form a barrier to their conception of the scheme therein so clearly expounded. For to the ordinary materialistic and intellectual man the conception of a Church is merely that of a human society, formed for the purpose of developing and carrying out of altruistic ideas by purely human methods, which, according to his bias, he either approves or disapproves of, or regards with indifference, but in no case looks upon as anything more than human; to such an one the idea of an interior Church, the soul or invisible guiding principle of that which is outwardly manifested, is not only fantastic in the extreme, but actually mischievous as importing a sanction which has no correspondence in reason or justice.

To the Churchman, on the other hand, who is familiar with the idea of an invisible Church, Eckartshausen's philosophy

does not accurately correspond to the theological conceptions
of the Church Waiting or of the Church Triumphant. He is
unfamiliar with the Eastern doctrine of the Seven Principles,
and he knows not that these, which he can find within himself,
and by the aid of trained intuition can examine and distinguish,
and reason about, can by analogy be postulated of every
created thing from the grain of dust to the mighty planey,
and even to the Kosmos itself; and that by the application of
this key it is possible to perceive, and even to prove, that the
Interior Church of Eckartshausen may coexist with the Church
Triumphant and the Church Waiting, and, indeed, not only
is no contradiction, but an actual proof of the reality of these
theological teachings.

Prejudice and preconception, however, will for a long time
keep both these classes of minds from giving a fair and unbiassed
study to the masterly exposition of the great German Mystic.
The small but steadily increasing class of occult students, who
are also Christians and Churchmen, will welcome these pages
at once, and will see without difficulty the wonderful analogies
opened out of the Church—the Mystic body of Christ to the
human body—and consequently the necessity for the existence
of various interior and invisible counterparts whereunto that
Body is perpetually striving to re-unite itself, even as the Man
is for ever striving to unite himself to his higher and divine
genius. He will see how that his own body, as well as the Mystic
Body of Christ, is in very deed the Temple of the Holy Ghost,
and how in each case there must rest a cloud on the Sanctuary
until the Body, which is the Church Militant, be re-united with
the original astral body, whose particles were drawn not only
from our human ancestors, nor only from this planet, but from
the justified and glorified souls of all God's sentient creation
throughout the Kosmos, whereof the Church, both visible and
invisible, is the material and outward expression, just as in
the Hebrew or Kabalistic system Nephesh is the expression of
Ruach, as Ruach is of Neshamah, and Malkuth is the vehicle
which outwardly manifests them all.

Seers and Clairvoyants, Prophets and Holy men of all ages, have been able to attain to actual certainty of these things, and to them the Communion of Saints is an open book. To such these ideas will offer no difficulty, but there are few to whom, in the same degree as Councillor Eckartshausen, has been given the power of expounding them clearly to ordinary men; and the English-speaking student is to be congratulated that Eckartshausen has found a translator at once so learned, both occultly and exoterically, and so sympathetic as the authoress of the following pages.

J. W. Brodie-innes

INTRODUCTION

THERE ARE MANY earthly sounds which are like the voice of the Spirit, but their insistence prevents us from hearing the true word which is being spoken in the houses of life. There are many urgent and clamorous representations in the name of the high interests which are not their accredited spokesmen, and it happens sometimes that a still, small voice speaking among them or on the outskirts—one that is heard scarcely—has a truer echo of the message which we are all longing to hear than those which speak with authority by the warrant of a common popular consent. To this second category belongs the Aulic Councillor Karl von Eckartshausen. Apart from *The Cloud upon the Sanctuary*, he is a name only to Christian mystics in England. He wrote much, and at his period and in his place he is said to have exercised some considerable influence; but his other works are quite unknown among us, while in Germany—though two or three have been reprinted—the majority seem practically forgotten, even among the special class to which some of them might be assumed to appeal. *The Cloud upon the Sanctuary* has, I believe, remained always in the memory of a few, and that it is destined still to survive I am very certain, for it is precisely one of those voices, heard in the quiet ways, to which I have just made reference—voices which speak of the deep and holy things as if they were native to the deeps, of the high things as if they came from the heights. To all who look within the body of religious doctrine for the true principle of life which energises the whole organism, this little book carries with it a message of great meaning. The present translation has offered it for the first time to English readers, and it enters now upon a further phase of existence. It appeared originally in the pages of *The Unknown World*, a magazine devoted to the fuller understanding of Christian mystical religion, and it was afterwards republished in separate form, of which there were two issues. In publishing it for the third time the lady who is responsible for the rendering has revised it there and here, and has authorised the inclusion of certain additional matter, so that perhaps it may approach finality. It has attracted considerable attention in England, and has deserved it; and although the work was translated into French from the original German in the year 1819, it has again appeared in that language, being redone in France from the English version, under the auspices of the late Countess of Caithness, for the pages of *L' Aurore*. These few words of bibliography are not unnecessary, because they establish the fact that there has been no inconsiderable sentiment of interest working within a restricted circle—as one may hope—towards the more general diffusion of a memorial which is at once suggestive from the literary standpoint—its imperfections of form notwithstanding—and profoundly moving on other and higher considerations. It encourages me to think that many persons who know and appreciate the tract already, or may come under its influence in the future, will learn with pleasure the little that I can tell them of its author, of two or three books of his own which connect therewith, and of some others—though not of his writing—which carry an analogous message, and the study of which may help us to understand its meaning.

Perhaps the most interesting thing that I can say at the beginning concerning Eckartshausen is that he relates to that group of mystics of which Lavater was so important a figure, the Baron Kirchberger an accomplished and engaging recorder, and Louis Claude de Saint-Martin a correspondent in France and an acknowledged source of leading. In his letters to Saint-Martin, Kirchberger says that Eckartshausen, with whom he was in regular communication by letter, was a man of immense reading and wonderful fertility; he regarded him in other respects as an extraordinary personage, "whatever way Providence may have led him." It would appear that at this period—namely, in 1795—Eckartshausen was seeking and deriving his chief light from the mystical study of numbers, but was also, to use the veiled and cautious language of the correspondence, in enjoyment of more direct favours. Saint-Martin confesses on his own part that he was more interested by Eckartshausen than he could express. Kirchberger must have held him in even higher estimation, and he undertook a journey to the Swiss frontier for the purpose of receiving from him the personal communication of the Lost Word; but an illness of the intending revealer frustrated this project. The point is of note because it establishes the pretensions of Eckartshausen. As to the Councillor of Berne so to us, he comes speaking with authority; and whatever may be our opinion about the kind of sacramentalism or economy which was involved in a proposal to communicate the Incommunicable Name—we shall get to understand presently the implication of this paradox—there are some of us who know, at least within certain limits, that the little book which I am introducing here puts forward no counterfeit claim. Saint-Martin acknowledges that part of the numerical system devised by Eckartshausen was in astonishing agreement with things that he had learned long ago in his own school of initiation—that of Martinés de Pasqually. Altogether the French mystic had formed the best opinion possible of his German brother, and his Swiss correspondent tells us further that Eckartshausen, although a courtier, walked in the narrow way of the inward life. In a letter to Kirchberger dated March 19, 1795, the philosopher by numbers bears witness to his personal experience, his instructions received from above, his consciousness of a higher presence, the answers which he had received and the visions, and the steps by which he had advanced even to the attainment of what he terms "the Law in its fulness." I have thought it well to give these data, derived from private letters, the publication of which was never designed or expected at the time, because they constitute a sketch of Eckartshausen taken to some extent unawares, when there could be the least reason to suppose that he was adopting an attitude.

His doctrine of the Interior Church must be interpreted by every one after his own lights; it is presented by himself as one having full knowledge and ambassadorial powers, as a voice speaking from the centre. My first and paramount purpose is to show that he was sincere, and this sincerity furnishes us with one more proof, out of proofs innumerable which are to be derived from other and independent sources, that things which are conceived in the heart when the heart is exalted to its highest can be realised in fine by the consciousness, and it is then that the new worlds open which are older than this world of ours. The sincerity of which I speak is, I think, illustrated by his life, which I will now summarise briefly.

Karl von Eckartshausen was born on June 28, 1752, at the Castle of Haimbhausen in Bavaria, and was the natural son of Count Karl of Haimbhausen by Marie Anne Eckhart, the daughter of the overseer of his estates. The mother died in giving birth to him, and he appears to have been a subject of the most solicitous affection on the part of his father, who educated him with the utmost pains. However, from the earliest years his illegitimacy is said to have filled him with almost unvaried melancholy and to have disposed him towards retirement from the world. At the same time, these characteristics—which were united to an amiable nature—endeared him to his family and friends. Through all his life he remained less or more a prey to the painful consequences of his original disqualification. He was destined notwithstanding to a career of some public importance. His first education was received at the college of Munich, and he proceeded afterwards to Ingolstadt for the study of philosophy and law, which he pursued with marked success. The university course at an end, his father procured him the title of Aulic Councillor; and in 1780 he was appointed censor of the library at Munich. This, in spite of the rectitude and goodness which characterised him, made him many enemies, but the favour of the Elector Karl Theodore sustained him against all combinations. In 1784 he was nominated Keeper of the Archives of the Electoral House, an appointment conferred, it is said, through a desire of the Elector to retain him near his person.

Eckartshausen published in all some sixty-nine works, embracing many classes of literature—the drama, politics, religion, history, art-criticism, general science, and, in particular, several contributions of varied merit to mystic and occult science. As indicated already, the majority of these are now forgotten, though some of his plays seem to have been successful in their day. *The Prejudice of Birth* in particular—his first printed drama—is described as abounding in felicitous situations and human interest. He attempted even a comedy, and this also received considerable approbation. One only of his books, under the title of *God is Purest Love*, commanded great and enduring popularity. Sixty editions are said to have been issued in Germany, and it was translated into most languages of Europe, as well as into Church Latin. It is a small collection of Catholic prayers and meditations on the love of God, the fear of God, the elevation of man's sentiments towards his Creator, the knowledge of the eternal, &c. There are also devotional exercises for use at Mass, before and after Confession, and at Communion, with acts of penance and acts of homage to the Blessed Virgin. In a word, I fail on my own part to see wherein or how far it differs from the innumerable manuals of piety which have been produced during the last two or three centuries for the use of the Catholic laity. I believe, however, that it still circulates in Germany, and it may even in France, where it had also a great vogue; it is held to possess a wonderful charm, though what is termed its intense mysticism is said to have puzzled some of its admirers. It has been described, indeed, as speaking the language and expressing the soul of Fenelon; but the value of this statement may be comparable to that of an opposite school of criticism, which has suggested that the religious philosophy is Deism veiled thinly. In any case, Eckartshausen—as I have intimated—wrote other and very different books—some on the Magic of Nature, some on the properties of numbers, and—as we shall have occasion to see shortly—he had entered into the chain of Hermetic tradition, and in at least one work he presented the metaphysical side of alchemy in language hitherto unheard. Finally, he was the author of *The Cloud upon the Sanctuary*, though the biographers to whom I am indebted for the facts and almost some words of the present notice have scarcely mentioned this late and crowning production of his intellectual life. In his private capacity he was amiable—as I have said—and charitable, devoting every month the result of his economies to the poor and his whole time to the practice of virtue. He was married three times, and left several children. He died on May 13, 1813 after a painful illness. The monographs of his period mention him as one of the best writers of Bavaria.

The point of view from which *The Cloud upon the Sanctuary* should be regarded is important from the claim which it makes. What is this Inner Church of which Eckartshausen speaks?—is a question which, I have said, must be answered by readers for themselves, according to their best direction. One thing which it is certainly not has been indicated by himself: it is no corporate body existing merely within the Church and controlling or leading it from a specific local centre in concealment. This possibility being negatived by the best of all authority on the subject, I should like on my own responsibility to negative also its most direct and clearest antithesis. It does not answer precisely to the collective mind or oversoul of the most advanced members of the visible Church, nor is it the official *consensus omnium sanctorum* which, according to the old Church maxim, is *sensus Spiritus Sancti*. Despite the absence of all corporate bonds, there is in the claim itself too direct a suggestion of conscious association occurring somehow in this present physical life. We must take the key which Eckartshausen himself offers, namely, that there is within all of us a dormant faculty, the awakening of which gives entrance, as it develops, into a new world of consciousness, and this is one of the initial stages of that state which he, in common with all other mystics, terms union with the Divine. In that union, outside all formal sects, all orthodox bonds of fellowship and veils and webs of symbolism, we shall form, or do form actually, a great congregation—the first fruits of immortality; and in virtue of the solidarity of humanity, and in virtue of the great doctrine of the communication of all things holy with all that seeks for holiness, the above and the below, this congregation is, in very truth—for I think that so much we can realise even in the normal understanding—the spirit of the visible Church of faith, aspiration and struggle, the Church Triumphant over-dwelling the Church Militant, and the channel through which the graces and benedictions of the Holy and Glorious Zion are administered to the Zion which is on earth.

Let us now illustrate the very strong claim which I have incorporated here in a paragraph by an analysis in detail—though this is also brief—which may be otherwise serviceable to readers as a summary of the work according to its chief purport. It is possible by seeking inwardly to approach the essential wisdom; and such wisdom is Jesus Christ, who is also the essence of love within us. The truth of this statement can be proved experimentally by any one, the condition of the experience being the awakening of a spiritual faculty for the cognition of spiritual objects as directly, substantially and naturally as the outward senses perceive natural phenomena. The organ in question is the intuitive sense of the transcendental world, and its awakening, which is the highest object of religion, takes place in three stages: (*a*) morally, by the way of inspiration; (*b*) intellectually, by the way of illumination; (*c*) spiritually, by the way of revelation. The awakening of this organ is the lifting of the Cloud from the Sanctuary, enabling our hearts to become receptive of God even in the present world. The knowledge of these mysteries has been preserved by an advanced school, illuminated inwardly by the Saviour, and perpetuated from the beginning of things to the present time. This Community is the Invisible Celestial Church, founded immediately after

the Fall and receiving a first-hand revelation for the raising
of humanity. But the weakness of men, as they multiplied,
necessitated an external society, namely, the Outward Church,
which, in the course of time, became separated from the Inner
Church, also through human weakness. The external Church
was consecrated originally in Abraham, but received its highest
perfection in the mystery of Jesus Christ. The Interior Church
is invisible, and yet, in some sense, governs all; it is perpetuated
in silence but in real activity, "and has united the science of the
Temple of the Ancient Alliance with the Spirit of the Saviour,"
or of the Interior Alliance. This Community of Light is the
union of all those capable of receiving light, and it is known
as the Communion of Saints. It possesses—in the most formal
words of Eckarthausen's claim—its school, its chair, its doctor,
a rule for students, with forms and objects of study, and, in
short, a method by which the study is pursued, together with
degrees for successive development to higher stages. We must
not, however, as I have said, regard it as a secret society, meeting
at certain times, choosing its elders and novices, for even the
chief does not invariably know all the members, while those
who are ripe for inclusion are joined to the body general when
perhaps they thought it least likely, and at a point of which they
knew nothing. The society constitutes a theocratic republic,
which one day will be the Regent-Mother of the whole world.
Its members are acquainted with the inmost heart of religions
and of the Holy Mysteries; but these treasures are concealed in
so simple a manner that they baffle unqualified research.

So far I have exposed the essential matter of the claim as
closely as possible in the words of him who is its messenger;
it is put forward by the way of affirmation, not by the way of
argument, and as such it is for those who have ears to hear a
message of this kind, because—in the nature of the case—there
is no evidence of the external kind. We have now to look at it
from a different standpoint, in a more individual manner, and
in the light which has been communicated otherwise to those

who are already mystics and initiated into the deeper meaning of the tradition which is from Christ.

I think that the testimony borne by Eckartshausen may be regarded under one of three aspects, but that two of them must be set aside in the end. There is the possibility—but here I have indicated already my personal doubt of this view—that he had been united with one of those secret fraternities of which there were so many at his period; and as some among such institutions were of a certain antiquity, there is no insuperable difficulty in supposing (*a*) that the particular association could have been an old one after its own kind, or (*b*) that it put forward a claim corresponding to that which would be made by a Secret Church. It is within possibility that a pretension of this sort might have been advanced in some quarters where secret tradition was perpetuated. Secondly, there is the possibility that as Eckartshausen had strenuously set his mature intellectual life on the higher side of holy thought in the Church, he may have attained an apprehension in the mystic consciousness which translated itself after this manner into his normal mind. There is, thirdly, the possibility that he gave expression in the terms of certitude to certain inferences of philosophical thought upon the history of religious belief and the experiences of religious life. I must put aside, at least for the moment, the last of these aspects because it involves an act of insincerity which—having regard to the nature of the claim—would not be less than grave, and of such an act—from all that we know of Eckartshausen—I believe that he was incapable. I set aside also, and definitely, the first because there are no traces of such a claim in associations, and it is too much and too arbitrary to assume it in the absence of a tolerable ground of presumption. Of Divine claims in traditional Secret Doctrine there is, of course, very full evidence; we meet with them in Kabalism and in Alchemy, but they are not put forward as a power or grace behind the Church, though they admitted in their respective degrees the Church of Israel and the Catholic Church of Christ. It remains, therefore, that through an experience in

the higher consciousness Eckartshausen entered into a certain
direct communion with that stream of tendency by which all
assemblies and all individuals that are seeking the Divine
do move in Divine directions—or, in other words, with the
leading of the Church and the soul. The possibility of such an
experience—outside all testimonies of the transcendental life—
can, I think, be made intelligible as an express realisation of the
spiritual mystery which is implied in the communion of saints,
to which Eckartshausen himself refers. This mystery can be
only understood as an integration of consciousness in common,
the unity of intelligence in its awakening to the actuality of
life in transcension, the intercourse of those who, without any
knowledge in the flesh, do meet—as we all meet—where there
is room for such meetings—namely, on the mountain heights. It
seems to me also that it translates itself readily into the normal
mind as a stage of that higher condition—highest indeed of
all—the *status unionis habitualis et actualis transformationis
animæ in Deum*. I suppose that these states are like those others
which are recognised by mysticism, that they occur by a kind
of intromission, and that the time for most is about half an
hour—that is, when there is silence in heaven. When it came
about that Eckartshausen—or another—decided to record that
which he had drawn from his experience within the logical
apprehension, he excogitated it subject to all normal limitations
from which he—or another—suffered, and he presented it as a
thesis which he was prepared to and did once argue out. It is in
this way that we find him at times too express in his statements,
as if he were dealing with an instituted assembly, and at others
leaving something unsaid—or hinted only—on the side of those
things which are vital to his own view.

The keynote of his entire thesis must be sought in his
comparison of the symbolical act of eating the Forbidden
Fruit with that mystical ordinance of the Church by which
Bread and Wine are communicated as flesh and blood of
Christ to the recipient of the Eucharist. It is, I think, a defect
of Eckartshausen that on this important subject he has given

only a vague hint and has left his general consideration in consequence retrenched or even dismembered. The deficiency works invidiously after two manners: it suggests an insufficient realisation on his own part of the Mystery which had been put into his hands, though I doubt that he could have reached so far as he did evidently if he had not used with success the one Key which does open the Sanctuary; alternatively, it suggests that he spoke as he could of certain secrets belonging to the inward life reserved in some instituted assembly, and this, on the grounds which I have attempted to allege already, I feel compelled to rule out of court, though it is that direction in which—by all my dispositions and more than all my environment—I lean naturally, while it is one, moreover, which would simplify the great issues.

The full consideration of the Eucharist in the Divine Degrees of its communication is impossible in this place, firstly, by the nature of my restrictions and, secondly, because I have dedicated *The Hidden Church of the Holy Graal* to this one subject, and in so far as it has been given me to speak at present thereon, I believe that I have exhausted everything. Let it be understood, therefore—and only—that the doctrine which can be formulated from the fruitful intimation of Eckartshausen is one which has not entered into the heart of dogmatic theology, yet it is one that theology will receive. The mystery of sin and evil was a mystery of communication in the deeps, while the mystery of grace and redemption was a mystery of communication in the heights, by which man is *ex hypothesi* restored to his first estate. To adapt some words of St. Augustine, we call the first—not because we are satisfied with the expression—the eating of the Forbidden Fruit, and the second we call—because we must have some expression—the communication of the body and blood of Christ to the flesh and the blood of our bodies.

There are three texts of Eckartshausen outside *The Cloud upon the Sanctuary* which may be said to connect therewith, and hence they demand passing or full reference in an attempt to introduce the most important of all his writings so that it shall be better understood in England. The first is a treatise on a new aspect of Chemistry, and it must be said here that he wrote more than once on this subject but not always from a standpoint of importance on the particular line of correspondence with which we are dealing now. The second is a little book called *Hieroglyphics*—in the sense of symbols and vestures belonging to the Sanctuary of the Heart; and the third is a curious *Catechism*—being part of a posthumous work entitled *The Magic of Nature*. This also is set forth as a *Catechism of the Higher Chemistry*, and in such respect, as in other ways, it recalls but is scarcely related to the other chemical treatises. Here it should be understood that the term is used in the sense of the mystic alchemist, Thomas Vaughan, when he derides those "who have pinned the narrow name of *Chemia* to a science both ancient and infinite." The chemistry of Eckartshausen is at times an excursion in the science of the soul, a synthetic account of the experiment which began, before the world was, with God, and is so continued *in sæcula sæculorum*—but there is no declaration of the term.

The *Catechism* is a clouded paradox, and though, because of its relationship, it might have been included as an appendix to *The Cloud upon the Sanctuary*, it would have required interpretation to an extent which here must have proved prohibitive. Assuming that *The Cloud upon the Sanctuary* is—as I have suggested—the record at a distance of things seen and heard in the higher consciousness, the *Catechism* is an attempt—comparatively speaking, secondhand—to rationalise more formally thereon—using for this purpose the unsuited, exploded and disdainful terminology of occult chemistry. As such, it is, I think, a failure. It tends, in the first place, to confuse the unversed mind by lending some colour to the supposition that, in speaking of the Holy Assembly, Eckartshausen refers to a community which has been organised on the material plane, and, as it answers also to some kind of an attributed name, may therefore have a species of local habitation. In this text he terms it more especially the Community of Light. But the informed reader will soon discern that he is allegorising in the averse sense, or—in other words—that he is translating things of the spirit into things—presumably equivalent—of human institution. He translates also the *Apostles' Creed*, the *Ten Commandments*, the *Pater noster*; the *Ave Maria*, the Corporal Works of Mercy, the Spiritual Works, the Counsels of Perfection, and so forth, into a kind of informal occult verbalism by which they profit in no wise. I register this criticism subject to a single important provision by way of reserve, arising out of a single reference which no one would notice in this obscure document, did I fail to draw attention thereto.

Let me say, therefore, that Eckartshausen's otherwise rather negligible *Credo* contains a root-principle of mystical philosophy which has not been made known publicly except therein. As an earnest of all that lies behind the *Catechism*, and is for the most part expressed so indifferently, it is not only encouraging to find one jewel deposited—as if undesignedly—on the surface, but incorporated in the Confession of Faith to explain in a few words the immanence of God in the phenomenal and Divine Providence as operating from the Divine Will manifested by a species of compulsion. The Articles of Faith are as follows: "I believe in creative Fire-Force, whence originated heaven and earth, *extensum* and *concretum*, the volatile and fixed. And in one Light, produced by this Fire-Force, ruler of the world, or of omnipotent power in Nature. This Pure Light, which proceeds from Fire, is received from the Purest Spirit and demitted into the purest form. BUT IT MUST SUFFER IN THE KINGDOM OF THE IMPURE; IT MUST BE DIVIDED, PUT TO DEATH AND BURIED IN THE EARTH. The Light then descends into the inmost being of matter, and after three epochs or three conjunctions of three spiritual forces with three purified forms, it is raised again into life, even to highest perfection, as a glorious force of Light, derived from Almighty Fire. And after this attainment it can make the dead alive and lead that which is imperfect to perfection. I believe in the Spirit of Light which proceeds from fire and warmth. I believe in the Community of Light, the communion of the followers of Light, the abolition of sickness and misery, the renewal of our being, and the final rapture of life."

I have exhibited by the device of capitals the brief clause which contains the Secret Doctrine, to which so many rites, ceremonies and legends of the instituted mysteries bear witness in their diverse manners. It is the cosmic side of the sacrifice consummated on Calvary in the world of the microcosm. By his possession of this teaching—from whatever quarter of the compass of thought it passed into his inheritance—we discern the justification of his paradoxical but abortive journey to meet Baron Kirchberger for the communication to the Swiss noble of the Lost Word. That Word—being not a verbal formula but the knowledge of the creative *Logos*—was, by the hypothesis of the Mysteries, concealed in the act of creation and its sepulchre is the material universe. After what manner the death and the entombment are alike mystical; after what manner the awakening occurs in the sanctuary to the prepared soul—these things remain the secrets of the sanctuary, though the collation of all that has been said sporadically, by accident or design, and is preserved in the records of the past, with the strange and growing intuitions of this our present time, seems to presage that *nihil tam occultum est quod non revelabitur*—and we know not when it may take place. For my own part, I will add upon this subject only three counsels of reflection as follows: (1) The term of rest in faith must be sought in the mystic annunciation that the Lamb was slain from the foundation of the world. (2) Even as Joseph of Arimathæa laid the body of Christ in a tomb which he had designed for himself, so does the high symbolism of Secret Doctrine proclaim after what manner God was buried in the sepulchre that was raised for man. (3) And in fine, as regards ourselves, if it were not for the grace of death, we should never be called to partake of the Great Resurrection.

Eckartshausen gives next in his *Catechism* the seven means or aids to attain the Light, and these would have been expressed better under their old names of the Seven Sacraments, because if he is speaking of things other than the paths of spiritual progress, his whole scheme is stultified; and if he is speaking of these, the old terms are the truest of all, and it is a wanton act to change them. Something furthermore would appear to have gone amiss with the mode of their enumeration, and I give them therefore in the more reasonable scheme required by their official analogies. *Baptism* is the preliminary and indispensable cleansing performed by water and the Word, to purify the matter and integrate it in the being of Light as a new and perfect body. It is therefore the qualification for entrance into the Kingdom of God—that is to say, the Holy Assembly. In *Confirmation* the matter is still further perfected by the chrism of Light and by the Spirit. The *Holy Eucharist* is that mystery of grace in which the principles of Bread and Wine are assumed by Light and the Word, when, as it is said, a Priest of Nature knows how to change these principles on the Altar. *Penance* is the work accomplished—also by a Priest of Nature—to remove the consequences of imperfection in matter which is susceptible of Light. *Extreme Unction* is the application of the Pure Light in the grade of perfect healing. *Holy Orders* are that state in virtue of which matter is consecrated by the operation of seven forces and is made receptive of Light. *Marriage* is the perfect union of Light with Fire by a medium. This reconstruction of the verbal form of sacramental doctrine is intelligible and almost simple as an attempt to present the stages of Christ's work in the soul, and the Secret Doctrine of the Eucharist emerges with comparative plainness, at least in its root-matter. As regards the Arch-Priest of Nature, we must deal herewith as we can, but must of all things be careful not to understand any earthly ministry, however consecrated, to remember that it is out of a mystic Salem that Melchizedek comes carrying Bread and Wine, and that the arch-natural host therefore descends from Heaven.

I do not deem it necessary to recite in their extension the Commandments of the Community of Light, which

are supposed to correspond with the *Decalogue*, but the
analogy is forgotten, with the result that there are three
precepts only, and the other clauses border on the ground of
doctrinal definition. As such, they leave much to be desired
on the score of correspondence between the expression and
intention, and much to be regretted in the needless recourse to
alchemical language. If we can tolerate these defects, however,
and the semi-pantheistic guise—which arises from verbal
confusion—the principle that is enunciated is one of order
and harmony in the work of spiritual progress and implicit
obedience to the laws which control the work. We have next
some commandments which correspond to those of the Church;
and here for the Annual Communion, which is imposed on the
faithful at Easter, according to the Latin obedience, it is weird
to meet the recommendation of a talk with a wise friend on
progress in the work. We have an attempted transliteration of
the *Pater noster*, for which I can concieve no tenable excuse,
and another of the *Ave Maria*, which speaks of the Light-Force
without conveying illumination. It should be said, however,
that the last rendering offers an analogy between the Virgin-
Mother of Christ and the Isis of Nature; which correspondence
is recognised in the instituted Mysteries; but is there extended
after a more intelligible manner. It is at this point again, and
indeed thenceforward through a number of lesser clauses, that
the student is likely to go astray, for the wording sounds like
the presentation of a physical experiment—as might be that
of metallic transmutation—in the terms of the science of the
soul, whereas the actual matter or subject is the formulation of
a spiritual experiment made by the inner man in the terms of
universal redemption. I pass over the enumeration of so-called
chemical sins, chemical counsels of perfection, corporal and
spiritual works which differ scarcely from their equivalents in
the *Latin Catechism*; and I will pause for a moment only at the
Eight Chemical Beatitudes, which—with a single exception, so
far unidentified—are simply excerpts from the *Apocalypse*, as,
for example: "He that overcometh shall not be hurt of the second

death," and "I will give him the morning star." They explain after what manner we are to understand the use of the word *Chemistry* in this tract by Eckartshausen, though the use is not justified thereby. I conceive that he was acquainted with the existence of the two schools—material and transcendental—in Alchemy, each represented by a literature which seems almost identical on the external sides. His intention may have been to illustrate in a paradoxical manner his adherence to the spiritual school and to direct the alchemists of his period—for a remnant still survived even in those days of disaster—to the brighter side—or that which he would have called the true object of an experiment known for several centuries under the evasive name of their Art. I must add in sincerity that the folly of the procedure remains, because it was and is legitimate to explain what the spiritual alchemists concealed under their strange terms, but it was not tolerable to perpetuate the use of this language at the beginning of the nineteenth century.

At the end of the *Catechism* Eckartshausen puts certain questions in the form of problems—paradoxes, again, of the Higher Science—and these he does not answer, but he offers in a final paragraph his theorem of Regeneration as follows: "The Inner Light is unknown, as such, to man, so long as he is not born of God—that is, so long as he regards things in his own mind, or in that of outward Nature, and not in the Divine." Our highest relations with God in this life are perhaps like those of a glass which reflects a perfect object gloriously, and it is only in certain moments that we reflect at our best—or at all. The reflection of things Divine in this *Catechism* suggests many intervening veils of cloud and mist. The last statement cited is certainly of all truth, yet I think that Eckartshausen has dealt with its special subject more luminously in *The Cloud upon the Sanctuary*.

The second of the three texts which connect with *The Cloud upon the Sanctuary* is Eckartshausen's *Most Important Hieroglyphics of the Heart of Man*, which has kinship with our purpose after two manners. It contains the doctrine of the

Interior Church at an earlier stage of its development in the mind of the writer, and it enables us to go back briefly to the last of the three aspects in which it is possible to regard his testimony as a whole. By those who refer to the original tract, the method of presentation will be found similar to that of *The Cloud* itself, and even verbal identity occurs here and there. In the first place Eckartshausen would dissuade his readers from concluding that his thesis in any sense makes void the External Church; for him, it was established by Christ, and it communicates the most holy arcana in common with the Church within, on which it depends, from which in a sense it draws, and wherein is the pledge indefectible, the plenary guarantee, of its truth. Those who deny the necessity of an External Church have deviated from the channel of communication, have forfeited the old trust, and, entering a false path, are liable at last to issue in materialism and Deism. *The Hieroglyphics of the Heart of Man*, like *The Cloud upon the Sanctuary*, is the work of a Catholic mind belonging to the Latin branch of official Christianity, and this branch was Eckartshausen's prototype throughout. As regards the Interior Church: (*a*) It has the title-deeds of all supersensual science and the primordial secrets declared therein; (*b*) it is invisible, but it rules everything; (*c*) its head is Jesus Christ; (*d*) it possesses the master-key by which biblical mysteries are opened, and the title-deeds which I have mentioned are actually the Bible itself; (*e*) as a community it is dispersed through the whole world and its members are joined in the interior for the erection of an eternal temple in the heart, where the Kingdom of God manifests; (*f*) the Interior Church subsists, therefore, in the heart and, apart from all conventions, each of its members takes his proper place therein; (*g*) in this manner he who is best and most worthy becomes thereby, *ipso facto*, the priest of the sanctuary and custodian-in-chief of the trust; (*h*) when it is said in *The Cloud* that the community draws its members from more than one world, the explanation is that the Interior Church extends beyond this material sphere, including the Holy Dead, the Angels of God, and finally Christ

Himself; (*i*) it is, therefore, in other words, distributed on the great ladder of the Hierarchy and is the archetype within of the Hierarchic Church without.

So far, as it seems to me, the earlier work represents only that which is expressed or implied in the later; but it will be seen by the enumeration which follows that it answers to what I have called an earlier stage of Eckartshausen's experience in the life within. He says: (1) Seeing that the Interior Church is the community of those who feel that the Kingdom of God is within them, it follows (2) that it lies in their own hands, by the development of this kingdom, to find the way of entrance into that Church; (3) the path is one of docility—even as in the soul of a child—of activity, faith, love, and of the hope which springs from these; (4) but after this stage there comes a deliverance of the spirit from the bonds of passion, with the appetites and false needs arising therefrom; (5) and, in fine, there is the grace communicated in prayer, in the study of Scriptural mysteries, and in the imitation of Christ. Now that—interpreted with proper understanding—all this is just, true and perfect, after its own manner, does not need illustration; but, I think, it is also clear that Eckartshausen had not as yet attained a sure criterion of distinction between the fruits which follow from the simple life of devotion—with interior but elementary recollection—and the deep and hidden ways of sanctity. Taken by themselves, these points seem to describe, under the misleading name of an Interior Church, a simple, fluidic unity or concurrence of disposition between pious persons in all ages, and within the bond of such union it would be folly to speak of a particular heritage in things concealed from the world or the direction of the external assemblies. The thesis, with all its strange, express and, indeed, categorical claims, could be reduced to a simple declaration of a concurrent harmony of mind in Christ Jesus apart from all consciousness in common. But it is a thesis of *The Cloud upon the Sanctuary* that there is a consciousness in common, and the work with which we are dealing presents, therefore, an early stage of the inquest. It is also a confused stage,

when that which he saw from afar was not fully understood by
the seer, who was, therefore, out of harmony with himse:f. It
is obvious from my previous extracts that *Hieroglyphics of the
Heart* is really trying to enunciate what we find more fully and
plainly in the later text. The author says, indeed—and, as one
may think, almost alternatively—that the entrance into the
Interior Church was facilitated in the Old Alliance through the
Law of Moses, in the New through the Christian Religion, but
that apart from external Churches there may be those who are
chosen out of other nations, though all indifferently are and can
be incorporated only through the Spirit of God. The distinction
and connection between that which is without and that which
is within are also shown clearly by the further statements
that the Outer and Inner Churches are joined through the
ceremonies, and that in this manner the Outer Church is so
guided that it cannot fall into error over the chief matters of
faith. In conclusion, as to this treatise, Eckartshausen discovers
in all schools of wisdom which can be traced in past ages, in
all ancient mysteries, a prevailing symbolism concerning a
House not made with hands, the attempt to externalise which,
producing a material building, is in one sense a false step, but
it has become a necessity through the operation of that mystery
which is termed the Fall of Man. It is unfortunate, however,
that Eckartshausen's attempted presentations of doctrine do
invariably a grave injustice to their essential merits. So far
from being synthetic or condensed, he suffers from a congenital
incapacity to say anything that he wishes clearly; he expends
himself consequently in abortive efforts, and amidst recurring
tautology and redundance it seems almost a mistake to translate
him, for that which he requires is re-expression.

I had intended in this place to say something at length
of Eckartshausen's contributions to that confused mystery
which he understood in the name of chemistry—apart from
what is contained in his *Catechism*; but an examination of
his chief work under the title of *New Chemistry* seems to
arrest its analysis, however briefly, as a thing that is remote

from our concern, negligible, as it has been always neglected, and forgotten, but not unjustly, if it can be said ever to have been known. As, further, it does not contain the preparatory *Meditation* before reading the letters of *The Cloud upon the Sanctuary*, I have been unable to identify the work from which that is extracted, though nothing attaches to the question. *Hieroglyphics of the Heart, Mystic Nights*, the not unpleasing parable called the *Travels of Kostis*—and I take here a few favourable samples out of a great collection of writings—may all be set aside profitably by those who would keep the memory of the *The Cloud upon the Sanctuary* untarnished in their heart. If there is anything that remains after such a drastic sifting, it is the little Treasury of Prayers to which I have already alluded. We can there kneel with the mystic when Mass is said at the altar; we can learn with what sentiments he received the Holy Eucharist, and after what manner he regarded the Lord of Glory as purest virtue and purest love hidden in the veil of mankind. Should it have—as it may perhaps have—a higher message for us than a few better known daily devotions, we shall not be without our reward; but apart from this—and speaking now intellectually—the connection will enable us to see more fully what is indeed so clear already: (*a*) that Eckartshausen, when he spoke of an External Church had but one institution in view; (*b*) that he spoke always from within it; (*c*) that he least of all would have held that advanced grades dispense from the sacraments; (*d*) that no trickeries of modern terminology—theosophical or otherwise—are applicable to any of his theses or exchangeable for his own language. He recognised at the same time that the institution of the External Church was destined to pass away, and he puts this very clearly in *Hieroglyphics*, but I judge from his other expressions that the time is that of consummation—being about that close of the ages when the Son shall yield up the Kingdom to the Father and God shall be all in all.

I think that this might well be taken as the term of our reflections, but I have promised to speak of certain books connecting with the claim of Eckartshausen, and perhaps in some measure assisting us further to get in touch with that claim. Unfortunately, in this restricted notice, I can do little more than name them. The first is *The Mystery of the Cross*, published originally in 1732—an anonymous work written in the French language, but—as it seems to follow from a statement of the writer—not the work of a Frenchman. It is an amiable and beautiful book, which, unknown to the world at large, has influenced many to their advancement and a few to some deeper understanding and fruition of hidden truth. Strangely embedded therein will be found several of the governing ideas and aspirations in schools of mystic thought which became illustrious in later years. The next book which I would note comes at first sight a little strangely in the professed connection, but it enters no less into the series; it is the dramatic poem of Ludwig Werner, having for its general title the name of *The Sons of the Valley*, but produced in two separable parts as *The Templars in Cyprus* and *The Brethren of the Cross*. It is the work of a man who was intimately acquainted with the mystic side of the Masonic movement at his period—that of the French Revolution—and a participant therein. The tradition embodied by Werner is the chivalrous tradition which had grown up in the high grades, and it is an interesting question—perhaps insoluble—how far he derived therefrom and how far his insight and genius may have helped to mould the tradition. After all his experience he carried his dreams and his knowledge into the fold of the Latin Church and became a priest. The two plays which constitute his poem convey many moving suggestions of a guiding but unknown hand influencing the Christian Church. The third book is of Russian origin, but was translated into French and published at Paris in 1801; of this translation a reprint was issued some few years since at Lyons. It is entitled *Some Characteristics of the Interior Church*; it connects the point of view met with in *The Mystery of the Cross* with that of Eckartshausen; it is interesting on account of its origin, and also for certain Martinistic associations, but it is less suggestive and much less developed. Finally, there is a remarkable and, I may add, a very rare series of works issued at Berleburg, in the province of Westphalia, in seven or more volumes, dated 1738. The first division is entitled *New Spiritual Discourses on various matters of the Interior Life and the Doctrines of the Christian Religion; or, Testimony of a Child of Truth concerning the ways of the Spirit*. These discourses occupy three volumes; two others contain a commentary on the *Apocalypse*; the sixth volume is a literal and mystical explanation of the *Epistle to the Romans*, with some supplementary papers and a *Catechism of the Science of Christian Religion*. The seventh volume—being the last that has come into my possession—is another commentary, verse for verse, on the first three chapters of *Genesis*. The collection as a whole may perhaps be described best as an appeal from external creeds, with their differences, their claims and their justifications, to the witness of the heart itself. It is an appeal also to the mystical doctors of the Church, and it cites many of the later mystics, from Tauler and Ruysbroeck to Engelbrecht, Antoinette de Bourignon and Madame Guyon. The discourses on the union of the Church of Christ and the spiritual union of the children of God, as also on a new Church, in the second volume, will be of interest to students of Eckartshausen. The keynote, perhaps, of the whole may be found in the *Explanation of the Epistle to the Romans* (vol. vi. pp. 143, 144), where it is said that the true universal Church is deeply concealed from the eyes of flesh, though its members may be members also—and that indifferently—of any one among the official communities. There are, in fine, extraordinary analogies with Saint-Martin, Eckartshausen and *The Mystery of the Cross*, to be found in the third volume, and having regard to the proximity of the date of publication to that of the last work, I incline to the opinion that there may have been some connection also in the authorship.

When these works have been studied, not in the letter only but in the spirit which is proper to their understanding, along with *The Cloud upon the Sanctuary*, the spiritual truths which

Eckartshausen has to some extent veiled, and his motives for so doing, may not be beyond discernment, nor the line of his experiences in all cases beyond pursuit.

Seeing now that, as we have found, Eckartshausen always remained in loyal communion with that External Church in which he was trained originally; seeing, therefore, that he did not regard apostasy and rebellion as among the first evidences of personal illumination; seeing that, like one of the Eastern teachers, he may have thought that some things could be changed from within, and this without haste, violence, or the altering of outward names and forms, it seems desirable to add that the thesis concerning the leading of the official Church by the Interior Church is that point where the testimony shows certain signs of breaking. We have already that doctrine of the Spirit which leads into all truth, so long as Its voice is heard; there is no colourable ground for replacing one by the other, and we should blaspheme our symbols did we say that the other was reinforced by the one. It is difficult to obtain an approximate comparative image; the leading is not the influence of a head upon the limbs which can be removed from a body; we must describe it rather as it is, namely, as the extra-sufficient grace on which natural grace does not depend presumably within its own measures, but which may be added thereto. When it is added, natural grace is transfused, though it does not cease to be. The root-matter of the lead must remain in the metal after its conversion into gold, on the hypothesis of physical alchemy; but, thus remaining, it is there in an undemonstrable state. So surely there is a higher part within us which overshadows our natural man when our normal being consents to that direction. We know it—but do we not?—in certain wonderful memorials. Yet we are not for that reason under a specific separable guidance; we are rather where all work together for the unity of all. Is it not after this manner that the secret church intervenes? I dream, but I do not know, except that we stand at a gate of high mysteries, and this is as near as we get to the special Providence exercised by the powers unseen.

The considerations with which we have been dealing are those which belong to eternity, and it remains for us now to conclude after the same manner, that there may be a blessing on all our work; that we may realise more fully, if this be needed, how the Voice of the Beloved is the horn of the great resurrection sounding over the sepulchres of the dead. Whether we speak of Eckartshausen or another in the annals of sanctity, it is only a peg on which to hang the high considerations of eternity. We have found that the reflection which is offered us in the glass of the German mystic is strange and beautiful and moving, but we have not found that it is perfect. We must, however, receive the gifts which are communicated to us by the official Churches and all the great literatures of the soul in the spirit which communicates, and we must ascribe to them on our part that sense in which we can understand them most fitly, so only that it is our highest sense. Thus are the dotations of all our ministers and brethren completed at need by our own. In this manner we consent to good doctrine as we consent to prudent economies, and there is shown a return on the investment which is thus secured to us for a season. It is increased in our hands, so that the capital is doubled in less than twenty years, and there is good business done in the spiritual Kingdom. We who have been collected into the middle palace of the mystics are therefore in the right refuge, and we are also under the charge of a royal master. We have placed our pledges of fidelity in the hands of a true legitimacy, and we know the King Whom we serve.

ARTHUR EDWARD WAITE

Advertisement Prefixed to the French Translation of 1819

A COLLECTION OF prayers entitled *God is Purest Love*, by the Councillor Eckartshausen, has been welcomed so cordially by the public that twenty editions have proved insufficient to satisfy the demands of its admirers. A success so extraordinary suggests that many of the same people would be interested in making acquaintance with the philosophy which inspired those Prayers. We can assure them that it will be found fully set forth in the present little volume by those who read it with the care which it deserves.

We refrain from expressing our personal opinion of the work, which may be called in a sense the Swan's Song of its author, who died shortly after its composition and by whom it was regarded as the general summary of his highest thoughts.

Regarding the fidelity of the translation, the confidence of the reader will no doubt be gained by the statement that we are perfectly familiar with the philosophical system contained herein and that we have left nothing untried to ensure that the sense of the writer is exactly respected.

A Short Method of Reflection

Before Reading

The Cloud upon the Sanctuary

Being an Extract from a Treatise on Chemistry
by Councillor Von Eckartshausen

*Si oculus tuus fuerit simplex totum corpus
tuum lucidum erit*—St. Luke ii. 34.

The interior eye of man is the higher reason: *potentia
hominis intellectiva, mens*. If this eye be illuminated by
Divine Light, then it is truly the inward Sun, by which all
things are made visible. So long as the Divine Light does not
enlighten this eye, there is internal darkness. When it shines,
there is morning within, for the Sun of the Soul shines in the
intellectual world, even as the external sun glorifies the world
without. When the external sun is lifted above the horizon, all
objects become visible gradually; and so at the rising of the
Spiritual Sun do the intellectual objects of the spiritual world
manifest by degrees in our consciousness. The light without
shows us the path of our pilgrimage and the Light within
reveals the way of salvation.

But as the external eye of man is subject to injury, so is the
interior eye liable also to dangers. It should be kept healthy, pure
and steady, and then—like the physical eye—it can be raised to
Heaven. As the one can gaze upon the firmament, the sun and
stars, so the other can contemplate all Heaven, the Angels and
God Himself—as it is said: *Signatum est super nos lumen vultûs*

tui (Ps. iv.): and *Ostendam omne bonum tibi* (Ex. vi. 33). What a glorious destiny is reserved for the man within!

The spiritual part of our being can be raised to the height of the angels and super-angelic intelligences; it can approach even the Throne of Divinity, beholding therein the magnificence of the Divine, spiritual and material worlds—as again it is written: *Averte oculum tuum, ne videat vanitatem.*

Withdraw, therefore, thy soul and thine inward eye from the things that are not of God; close up thyself from the night of error and of prejudice; open thyself only to the Spiritual Sun. That Sun is Jesus Christ! As from the earthly sun proceed light and heat, revealing all objects, causing growth and fruition in everything, so does the Inward Sun reveal all things to the mind, raise all to activity in the heart, because Wisdom and Love are His powers, while our reason and will are His organs. He strengthens our forces with Wisdom and our Wills with Love.

ON THE DEVELOPMENT OF HUMAN FORCES

In proportion as a body is organised the more fully for the reception, development and propagation of diverse influences, so is its existence the richer and more perfect, because there is greater vital capacity. But many powers may remain dormant within us, because there are no organs for their manifestation. Such sleeping powers can, however, be awakened—that is to say, we can so organise ourselves that the forces can become active within us.

An organ is a certain form wherein a force acts, but every form consists in the determinate direction of its parts towards the operating force. By organising oneself for the due action of a force, there is meant simply that such form and situation are given to the parts as will enable the force to act therein. This is the state of organisation. But as the light which does not exist for a man who has no eyes is enjoyed by all but the blind, so there are men who can enjoy gifts which are unknown to many. I mean to say that one man will see, hear, feel and taste things of which another has no experience because the requisite organs are in him lacking. In such a case, explanations are useless, seeing that the deficient person will identify any testimony which the other may bear with the notions which he has received from his particular organism, because he can understand it only in so far as it corresponds to his sensations.

As we receive ideas through our senses and as all the operations of our reason are abstractions of sensible impressions, it is clear that there are many things of which we can form no conception because we have as yet no sensation thereof. That only for which we have organised capacity becomes for us apparent. Hence it seems clear that those who are organised for the development of higher forces cannot convey to those who are not so organised more than a vague idea of the greater truth. Hence also our disputes and contentions serve little purpose: man first rust be organised for the reception of truth. We might publish great treatises on light, but the blind could not see by their help; they must first have the seeing eye.

The question therefore is: Wherein consists the necessary organ for beholding truth and what is the capacity for such in man?

I answer: In simplicity of heart; for simplicity places the heart in a suitable position to receive unrefracted the light of reason, and it is this which organises the heart for the reception of Light.

THE CLOUD
UPON THE SANCTUARY

LETTER I

THERE is no age more remarkable to the quiet observer than our own. Everywhere there is a fermentation in the mind, as in the heart of man ; everywhere there is a battle between light and darkness, between exploded thought and living ideas, between powerless wills and living active force ; in fine, everywhere there is war between animal man and growing spiritual man.

It is said that we live in the age of light, but it would be truer to say that we are living in that of twilight ; here and there a luminous ray pierces the mist of darkness, but does not light to full clearness either our reason or our heart. Men are not of one mind, scientists dispute, and where there is discord, truth is not yet apprehended.

The most important objects for humanity are still undetermined. No one is agreed either on the principle of reason, on the principle of morality, or on the cause of the will. This proves that though we are dwelling in a reputed age of light, we do not well understand what emanates from our hearts—and what from our heads. Probably we should reach this knowledge much sooner if we did not imagine that we have the torch of science already in our hands, or if we would cast a look on our weakness and recognise that we need a higher illumination. We live in the times of idolatry of the intellect; we place a common light upon the altar and we loudly proclaim that here and now is the aurora, that everywhere daylight is really about to appear, and that the world is emerging more and more from obscurity into the full day of perfection, through the arts, sciences, cultured taste, and even by a purer understanding of religion.

Poor mankind! To what eminence have you raised the happiness of man? Has there ever been an age which has counted so many victims to humanity as the present? Has there ever been an age in which immorality and egotism have been greater or more dominant than in this one? The tree is known by its fruits. Insensate beings! With your imaginary natural reason, from whence have you the light by which you are so willing to enlighten others? Are not all your ideas borrowed from your senses, which do not give you the reality but merely its phenomena? Is it not true that in time and space all knowledge is but relative? Is it not true that all which we call reality is also relative, for absolute truth is not to be found in the phenomenal world. Thus your natural reason does not possess the true essence, but only an appearance of truth and light ; and the more this semblance increases and spreads, the more the essence of light fades inwardly ; the man is lost in the apparent and gropes vainly after dazzling phantasmal images devoid of all actuality.

The philosophy of our age raises the natural intellect into independent objectivity, gives it judicial power, exempts it from any superior authority, makes it autonomous, converting it into divinity by closing all harmony and communication with God ; and deified Reason, which has no other law but its own, is to govern Man and make him happy! Can darkness spread the light? . . . Can poverty dispense wealth? Is death capable of giving life?

It is truth which leads man to happiness. Can you confer truth?

That which you call truth is a form of conception empty of real matter ; its knowledge is acquired from without, through the senses, and the understanding co-ordinates these by observed synthetic relationship into science or opinion.

You abstract from the Scriptures and Tradition their moral, theoretical and practical truth ; but as individuality is the principle of your intelligence, and as egotism is the incentive to your will, you do not see, by your light, the moral law which dominates, or you repel it with your will. It is to this length that the light of to-day has penetrated. Individuality under the cloak of false philosophy is a child of corruption.

Who can pretend that the sun is in full zenith if no bright rays illuminate the earth, and no warmth vitalises vegetation? If wisdom does not benefit man, if love does not make him happy, but very little has been done for him on the whole.

Oh! if only natural man, that is, sensuous man, would learn that the principle of his reason and the incentive of his will are only his individuality, and that on this account he is miserable, he would then seek interiorly for a higher principle, and he would thereby approach that source which alone can communicate this principle to all, because it is *wisdom in its essential substance.*

Jesus Christ is Wisdom, Truth and Love. He, as Wisdom, is the Principle of reason and the Source of the purest knowledge. As Love, He is the Principle of morality, the true and pure incentive of the will.

Love and Wisdom beget the spirit of truth, the interior light; this light illuminates us and makes supernatural things objective to us.

It is inconceivable to what depths of error a man falls when he abandons simple truths of faith by opposing his own opinions.

Our century seeks to determine by subtlety of brain the principle of reason and morality, or the ground of the will; if the men of science were mindful, they would see that these things are better answered in the heart of even the simplest man than through their most brilliant casuistry. The practical Christian finds the incentive of the will, the principle of all morality, really and objectively in his heart; and this incentive is expressed in the following formula:—" Love God with all thy heart, and thy neighbour as thyself."

The love of God and his neighbour is the motive for the Christian's will, and the essence of love itself is Jesus Christ dwelling within us.

It is in this way that the principle of reason is wisdom in us; and the essence of wisdom—wisdom in its substance—is again Jesus Christ, the light of the world. Thus we find in Him the principle of reason and of morality.

All that I am now saying is not hyperphysical extravagance; it is reality, absolute truth, that every one can prove for himself by experience, as soon as he receives within him the principle of all reason and morality—Jesus Christ, being wisdom and love *in essence*.

But the eye of the man of sensuous perception only is closed firmly to the fundamental basis of all that is true and all that is transcendental.

Even that reason which many would fain raise to the throne of legislative authority is only reason of the senses, whose light differs from that of transcendental reason, as does the phosphorescent glimmer of decayed wood from the glories of sunshine.

Absolute truth does not exist for sensuous man ; it exists only for interior and spiritual man who possesses a suitable sensorium ; or, to speak more correctly, who possesses an interior organ to receive the absolute truth of the transcendental world, a spiritual faculty which cognises spiritual objects as objectively and naturally as the exterior senses perceive external phenomena.

This interior faculty of the man spiritual, this sensorium for the metaphysical world, is unfortunately not yet known to those who cognise only on the external, for it is a mystery of the kingdom of God.

The current incredulity towards everything which is not cognised objectively by our senses explains the present misconception of truths which are, of all, most important to man.

But how can this be otherwise ? In order to see one must have eyes, to hear one must have ears. Every apparent object requires its appropriate senses. So also transcendental objects require their sensorium—and it is this sensorium which is closed in most men. Hence they judge the metaphysical world through the intelligence of their senses, even as the blind imagine colours and the deaf judge tones—without suitable instruments.

There is an objective and substantial ground of reason, an objective and substantial motive for the will. These two together form the new principle *of life*, and morality is there essentially inherent. This pure substance of reason and will, re-uniting in us the Divine and the human, is Jesus Christ, the light of the world, who must enter into direct relationship with us, to be really recognised.

This real knowledge is actual faith, in which everything takes place in spirit and in truth.

We must therefore have a sensorium fitted for such communication, an organised and spiritual sensorium, a spiritual and interior faculty able to receive this light; but it is closed—as I have said—to most men by the incrustation of the senses.

Such an interior organ is the intuitive sense of the transcendental world, and until this intuitive sense is effective in us we can have no certainty of more lofty truths. This organism has been naturally inactive since the Fall, which relegated man to the world of physical sense. The gross matter which envelops the interior sensorium is a film which veils the internal eye, and prevents the exterior eye from seeing into spiritual realms. This same matter muffles our internal hearing, so that we are deaf to the sounds of the metaphysical world; it so paralyses our spiritual speech that we can scarcely stammer words of sacred import, *words which we pronounced formerly*, and by virtue of which we held authority over the elements and external nature.

The opening of this spiritual sensorium is the mystery of the New Man—the mystery of Regene-

ration, and of the vital union between God and man
—it is the noblest object of religion on earth, of that
religion whose sublime goal is none other than to
unite men with God in Spirit and in Truth.

We can discern easily after this manner why it is
that religion tends always towards the subjection of
the senses. It does so because it desires to make the
spiritual man dominant, in order that the truly
rational man may govern the man of sense. Philosophy feels this truth, only its error consists in
not apprehending the true source of reason, and in
attempting to replace it by individuality and sensuous reason.

As man has internally a spiritual organ and a
sensorium to receive the true principle of reason,
or divine wisdom, and a true motive for the will, or
divine love, so he has likewise exteriorly a physical and
material sensorium to receive the *appearance* of light
and truth. As external nature can have no absolute
truth, but only the relative truth of the phenomenal
world, so human reason cannot cognise intelligible
truth ; it can but apprehend through the appearance
of phenomena, which stimulate concupiscence only
as a motive for the will, and in this consists the
corruption of sensuous man and the degradation
of nature.

The exterior sensorium in man is composed of
frail matter, whereas the internal sensorium is
organised fundamentally from incorruptible, transcendental and metaphysical substance.

The first is the cause of our depravity and our mortality, the second of our incorruptibility and of our immortality.

In the regions of material and corruptible nature mortality hides immortality; therefore all our trouble results from corruptible mortal matter. In order that man should be released from this distress, it is necessary that the immortal and incorruptible principle, which dwells within, should expand and absorb the corruptible principle, so that the envelope of the senses should be removed, and man appear in his pristine purity.

This natural envelope is a truly corruptible substance found in our blood, forming the fleshly bonds binding our immortal spirits under the servitude of the mortal flesh.

This envelope can be rent more or less in every man, and then he can be placed in greater spiritual liberty, and can be made cognisant of the transcendental world.

There are three different degrees in the opening of our spiritual sensorium.

The first degree reaches to the moral plane only; the transcendental world then operates in us by interior movements, called inspiration.

The second and higher degree opens our sensorium to the reception of the spiritual and the intellectual, and then the metaphysical world *works* in us by interior *illumination*.

The third degree, which is the highest and most

seldom attained, opens the whole inner man. It breaks the crust which darkens our spiritual eyes and ears; it reveals the kingdom of spirit, and enables us to see, objectively, metaphysical and transcendental sights; hence all visions are explained fundamentally.

Thus we have an internal sense of objectivity as well as that which is external; but the objects and the senses are different. Exteriorly animal and sensual motives act in us and corruptible sensuous matter receives the action. Interiorly it is metaphysical and indivisible substance which gains admittance within, and the incorruptible and immortal essence of our Spirit receives its influence. Nevertheless, generally things pass much in the same way interiorly as they do externally. The law is everywhere the same. Hence—as the spirit or our internal man has far other senses and another objective sight than the rational man—one need not be surprised that the spirit should remain an enigma for the scientists of our age, for those who have no objective sense of the transcendental and spiritual world. They measure the supernatural by the measurement of the senses; they confound the corruptible motive with the incorruptible substance, and their judgments are necessarily false on an object for the discernment of which they possess no senses, no objectivity of the thing in consequence, and—also in consequence—neither relative nor absolute truth. So far, however, as regards those truths which we proclaim herein, we owe a debt of gratitude towards the philosophy of Kant.

Kant has shown incontestably that the natural reason can know absolutely nothing of what is supernatural, spiritual and transcendental; that it can understand nothing either analytically or synthetically; and that thus it can neither prove the possibility nor the reality of spirits, or souls, or God.

This is a great truth, lofty and beneficial for our epoch, though it is obvious that St. Paul has already enunciated it (1 Cor. i. 2–24). But the pagan philosophy of Christian scientists has been able to ignore it up to Kant. The increment of this truth is dual: in the first place, it puts insurmountable limits to the sentiment, to the fanaticism and to the extravagance of carnal reason. Secondly, it shows, by dazzling contrast, the necessity and divinity of Revelation. It proves that our human reason, in its state of enfoldment, *has no* objective source for the supernatural except revelation, no source otherwise of instruction in Divine things or concerning the spiritual world, the soul and its immortality; hence it follows that without revelation it is absolutely impossible to suppose or conjecture anything regarding these matters.

We are, therefore, indebted to Kant for proving philosophically, nowadays, what long ago was taught in a more advanced and illuminated school—*that without Revelation no knowledge of God, neither any doctrine touching the soul, could be at all possible.*

It is therefore clear that an universal Revelation must serve as a fundamental basis to all mundane religions.

Hence, following Kant, it is çlear that the intelligible world is wholly inaccessible to natural reason, and that God dwells in light, into which no speculation of the enfolded reason can penetrate. Thus the natural man, or man of human reason, has no sense of transcendental reality, and therefore it was necessary that it should be *revealed* to him, for which faith is required, because the means are given to him in faith whereby his inner sensorium unfolds, and through this he can apprehend the reality of truths otherwise incapable of being understood by the natural man.

It is quite true that with new senses we can acquire the perception of further reality. This reality exists already, but it is not known to us, because we lack the organ by which to cognise it. One must not lay blame on the percept, but on the receptive organ.

With, however, the development of the new organ we have a new perception, a sense of new reality. In its absence the spiritual world cannot exist for us, because the organ rendering it objective to us is not developed. In its unfoldment, the curtain is all at once raised, the impenetrable veil is torn away, the cloud before the Sanctuary lifts, a new world suddenly exists for us, scales fall from the eyes, and we are transported from the phenomenal world to the regions of truth.

God alone is *substance*, absolute truth; He alone is He who *is*, and we are what He has made us. For Him, all exists in Unity; for us, all exists in multiplicity.

A great many men have no more idea of the development of the inner sensorium than they have of the true and objective life of the spirit, which they neither perceive nor forecast in any manner. Hence it is impossible for them to know that one can comprehend the spiritual and transcendental, and can thus be raised to the supernatural, even to vision thereof.

The great and true work of building the Temple consists solely in destroying the miserable Adamic hut and in erecting a divine temple; this means, in other words, to develop in us the interior sensorium, or the organ to receive God. After this process, the metaphysical and incorruptible principle rules over the terrestrial, and man begins to live, not any longer in the principle of self-love, but in the Spirit and in the Truth, of which he is the Temple.

The moral law then evolves into love for one's neighbour in deed and in truth, whereas for the natural man it is but a simple attitude of thought; the spiritual man, regenerated in spirit, sees all that *in its essence* of which the natural man has only the forms void of thought, mere empty sounds, symbols and letters, which are dead images without interior spirit. The most exalted aim of religion is the intimate union of man with God; and this union is possible here below; but it can only take place by the opening of our inner sensorium, which enables our hearts to become receptive of God.

Therein are those great mysteries of which our human philosophy does not dream, the key to which is not to be found in scholastic science.

Meanwhile, a more advanced school has always existed to which the deposition of all science has been confided, and this school was the community illuminated interiorly by the Saviour, the society of the Elect, which has continued from the first day of creation to the present time; its members, it is true, are scattered all over the world, but they have always been united by one spirit and one truth; they have had but one knowledge, a single source of truth, one lord, one doctor and one master, in whom resides substantially the whole plenitude of God, who also alone initiates them into the high mysteries of Nature and the Spiritual World.

This community of light has been called from all time the invisible and interior Church, or the most ancient of all communities, of which we will speak more fully in the next letter.

LETTER II

IT is necessary, my dear brothers in the Lord, to give you a clear idea of the interior Church; of that illuminated Community of God which is scattered throughout the world, but is governed by one truth and united in one spirit.

This community of light has existed since the first day of the world's creation, and its duration will be to the end of time. It is the society of those elect who know the Light in the Darkness and separate what is pure therein.

This community possesses a School, in which all who thirst for knowledge are instructed by the Spirit of Wisdom itself; and all the mysteries of God and of nature are preserved therein for the children of light. Perfect knowledge of God, of nature and of humanity are the objects of instruction in this school. It is thence that all truths penetrate into the world; herein is the School of the Prophets and of all who search for wisdom; it is in this community alone that truth and the explanation of all mystery is to be found. It is the most hidden of communities, yet it possesses members gathered from many orders; of such is this School. From all time there has been an exterior school based on the interior one, of which it is but the outer expression. From all time, therefore, there has been a hidden assembly, a society of the Elect, of those who sought for and had capacity for light, and this interior society was called the interior Sanctuary or Church. All that the external Church possesses in symbol, ceremony or rite is the letter which expresses externally the spirit and the truth residing in the interior Sanctuary.

Hence this Sanctuary, composed of scattered members, but knit by the bonds of perfect unity and love, has been occupied from the earliest ages in building the grand Temple to the regeneration of humanity, by which the reign of God will be manifest. This society is in the communion of those who have most capacity for light, *i.e.*, the Elect. The Elect are united in spirit and in truth, and their Chief is the Light of the World Himself, Jesus Christ, the One Anointed in light, the single mediator for the human race, the Way, the Truth and the Life— Primitive Light, wisdom and the only *medium* by which man can return to God.

The interior Church was formed immediately after the fall of man, and received from God at first-hand the revelation of those means by which fallen humanity could be again raised to its rights and delivered from its misery. It received the primitive charge of all revelation and mystery ; it received the key of true science, both divine and natural.

But, when men multiplied, the frailty of man and his weakness necessitated an exterior society which veiled the interior one, and concealed the spirit and the truth in the letter. The people at large were not capable of comprehending high interior truth, and the danger would have been too great in confiding that which was of all most holy to incapable people. Therefore, inward truths were wrapped in external and visible ceremonies, so that men, by the perception of the outer, which is the symbol of the interior, might by degrees be enabled safely to approach the interior spiritual truths.

But the secret depository has always been confided to him who in his day had the most capacity for illumination, and he became the sole guardian of the original Trust, as High Priest of the Sanctuary.

When it proved necessary that interior truths should be enfolded in exterior ceremony and symbol, on account of the real weakness of men who were not capable of sustaining the unveiled Light, then exterior worship began. It was, however, always the type and symbol of the interior—that is to say, the symbol of the true homage offered to God *in spirit* and *in truth*.

The difference between spiritual and animal man, or between rational and sensual man, made the exterior and interior imperative. Interior truth passed into the external wrapped in symbol and ceremony, so that sensuous man could observe and be led gradually thereby to interior truth. Hence external worship

3

was symbolically typical of interior truths, of the relationship between man and God before and after the Fall, the estate of his dignity and of his most perfect reconciliation. All the symbols of external worship are based upon the three fundamental relations—the Fall, the Reconciliation and the Complete Atonement.

The care of the external service was the occupation of priests, and every father of a family was in the ancient times charged with this duty. First fruits and the first born among animals were offered to God, the one symbolizing that all which preserves and nourishes us comes from Him; the other that animal man must be killed to make room for rational and spiritual man.

The external worship of God should never have been separated from interior service, but as the weakness of man tended too easily to forget the spirit in the letter, so the Spirit of God was vigilant to note in every nation those who had most capacity for light; they were employed as agents to spread the light according to man's capacity, and to revivify the dead letter by the Spirit and the truth.

Through these divine instruments the interior truth of the Sanctuary was taken into all nations, and modified symbolically according to their customs, capacity for culture, climate and receptiveness. So therefore the external types of every religion, worship, ceremonies and Sacred Books in general have more or less clearly, as their object of instruction, the

interior truths of the Sanctuary, by which man—
but only in the latter days—will be conducted
to the universal knowledge of the one Absolute
Truth.

The more the external worship of a people has
remained united with the spirit of esoteric truth, the
purer its religion ; but the wider the difference has
been between the symbolic letter and the invisible
truth, the more imperfect has become the religion.
It even degenerated into polytheism among some
nations, when the external letter lost utterly the
interior spirit, when the external form parted entirely
from its inner truth, when ceremonial observances
without soul or life remained alone.

When the *germs* of the most important truths had
been carried everywhere by God's agents, He chose
a certain people to raise up *a vital symbol* destined
to manifest the means by which He intended to
govern the human race in its present condition, and
by which it would be led into complete purification
and perfection.

God Himself communicated to this people its
exterior religious legislation ; He gave all the symbols
and enacted all the ceremonies, and they contained
the impress, as it were, of the great esoteric truths of
the Sanctuary.

God consecrated this external Church in Abraham,
gave its commandments through Moses, and thereto
assured its highest perfection by the dual mission of
Jesus Christ, existing personally in poverty and

suffering, and by the communication of His Spirit in the glory of the Resurrection.

Now, as God Himself laid the foundation of the outer Church, the whole of the symbols of external worship formed the science of the Temple, or of the Priests, in those days, and the mysteries of the most sacred truths became external through revelation. The scientific knowledge of this holy symbolism was the science designed to unite fallen man once more with God; hence religion received its name from being the science of rebinding man with God, to bring man back to his origin.

One sees plainly by this pure idea of religion in general that the unity thereof is to be sought in the inner Sanctuary, and that the multiplicity of external religions can never alter the true identity which is at the base of every exterior.

The wisdom of the temple under the ancient alliance was preserved by priests and by prophets. To the priests was confided the external,—the cortex of hieroglyph. The prophets had the charge of the inner truth, and their occupation was continually to recall the priests from the letter to the spirit when they began to forget the spirit and cleave only to the letter. The science of the priests was that of the knowledge of exterior symbols. That of the prophets was experimental possession of the truth of the symbols. In the external was the letter; in the interior the spirit lived. There was, therefore, in the ancient alliance a school of prophets and of priests, the one occupying itself with the spirit in the emblem, the other with the emblem itself. The priests had the external possession of the Ark, of the shew-bread, of the candlestick, of the manna, of Aaron's rod; but the prophets were in interior possession of the inner spiritual truth which was represented exteriorly by the symbols just mentioned.

The external Church of the ancient alliance was visible; the interior Church was always invisible, must be invisible, and yet must govern all, because force and power are alone confided to her.

When the divine, external worship abandoned the interior worship, it fell, and God proved by a remarkable chain of circumstances that the letter could not exist without the spirit, that it is only there to lead to the spirit, and that it is useless and even rejected by God if it fails in this object.

As the spirit of nature extends to the most sterile depths to vivify, preserve and cause growth in everything susceptible of its influence, so also the spirit of light spreads itself interiorly among nations to animate everywhere the dead letter by the living spirit.

This is why we find a Job among idolaters, a Melchizedek among strange nations, a Joseph with the Egyptian priests, a Moses in the country of Midian, as living proofs that the interior community of those who are capable of receiving light was united by one spirit and one truth in all times and among all nations.

To these agents of light from the one inner
community was united the Chief of all agents, Jesus
Christ Himself, in the midst of time, as *royal priest*
after the order of Melchizedek.

The divine agents of the ancient alliance hitherto
represented only specialised perfections of God;
therefore a powerful movement was required which
should show all at once—*all in one*. An universal
type appeared, which gave the real touch of perfect
unity to the picture, which opened a fresh door and
destroyed the number of human bondage. The law
of love began when the image emanating from
wisdom itself showed to man all the greatness of
his being, vivified him anew, assured him of his
immortality, and raised his intellectual status that
it might become the true temple for the spirit.

This Chief Agent of all, this Saviour of the World
and universal Regenerator, claimed man's whole
attention to the primitive truth, whereby he could
preserve his existence and recover his former dignity.
Through the conditions of His own abasement He
laid the foundation of the redemption of man, and
He promised to accomplish it completely one day
through His Spirit. He showed also truly in a
narrower circle—that is, among His apostles—those
things which should come to pass in the future to
all the Elect.

He extended the chain of the inner community of
light among His Elect, to whom He sent the Spirit
of Truth, and confided to them the most exalted

primitive instruction in all divine and natural things as a sign that He would never forsake His community.

When the letter and symbolic worship of the external Church of the ancient alliance had been realised by the Incarnation of the Saviour, and verified in His person, new symbols became requisite for external use, which showed us through the letter the future accomplishment of universal redemption.

The rites and symbols of the external Christian Church were formed after the pattern of the great, unchangeable and fundamental truths, announcing things of a strength and of an importance impossible to describe, and revealed only to those who knew the innermost Sanctuary.

This Sanctuary remained changeless, though external religion received in the course of time and circumstances varied modifications, and became divorced from the interior truths which can alone preserve the letter. The profane idea of wishing to "secularize" all that is Christian, and to Christianise all that is political, changed the exterior edifice, and covered with the shadow of death all that reposed within it of light and life. Hence rose divisions and heresies, and the spirit of Sophistry ready to expound the letter when it had already lost the essence of truth.

Current incredulity increased corruption to its utmost point, attacking the edifice of Christianity in its fundamental parts, confusing the sacred interior with the exterior, already enfeebled by the ignorance of weak man.

Then was born Deism; this brought forth materialism, which looked on the union of man with superior forces as imaginary; then finally came forth, partly from the head and partly from the heart, the last degree of man's degradation—Atheism.

In the midst of all this, truth reposed inviolable in the inner Sanctuary.

Faithful to the spirit of truth, which promised never to abandon its community, the members of the interior Church lived in silence, but in real activity, and united the science of the temple of the ancient alliance with the spirit of the great Saviour of man—the spirit of the interior alliance—waiting humbly the great moment when the Lord will assemble His community in order to give every dead letter external force and life.

This interior community of light is the reunion of all those capable of receiving light, and elect thereto; it is known as the *Communion of Saints*. The primitive deposit of all power and truth has been confided to it from all time—it alone, says St Paul, is in the possession of the science of the Saints. By it the agents of God were formed in every age, passing from the interior to the exterior, and communicating spirit and life to the dead letter —as already said.

This illuminated community has been through time the true school of God's spirit, and considered as school, it has its Chair, its Doctor, it possesses a rule for students, it has forms and objects for study, and, in short, a method by which they study.

It has, also, its degrees for successive development to higher altitudes.

The first and lowest degree consists in the moral good, by which the simple will, subordinated to God, is led to good by the pure motive of the will which is Jesus Christ, received by faith. The means by which the spirit of this school acts are called inspirations.

The second degree consists in that rational intellectuality by which the understanding of the man of virtue, who is united to God, is crowned with wisdom and the light of knowledge, and the means which the spirit uses to produce this are called interior illumination.

The third and highest degree is the entire opening of our inner sensorium, by which the inner man attains the objective vision of real and metaphysical verities. This is the highest degree, when faith passes into open vision, and the means which the spirit uses to this end are real visions.

Such are the three degrees of the school for true interior wisdom—that of the illuminated Society. The same spirit which ripens men for this community also distributes its degrees by the co-action of the ripened subject.

This school of wisdom has been for ever most secretly hidden from the world, because it is invisible and submissive solely to Divine Government.

It has never been exposed to the accidents of time and to the weakness of man, because only the most capable were chosen for it, and the spirit which selected could suffer no deception.

By this school were developed the germs of all the sublime sciences, which were next received by external schools, were then clothed in other forms, and in fine sometimes degenerated therein.

This society of sages communicated, according to time and circumstances, unto the exterior societies their symbolic hieroglyphs, in order to attract external man to the great truths of the interior.

But all exterior societies subsist only in proportion as this society communicates its spirit thereto. As soon as external societies wish to be independent of the interior one, and to transform a temple of wisdom into a political edifice, the interior society retires and leaves only the letter without the spirit. It is thus that secret external societies of wisdom were nothing but hieroglyphic screens, the truth remaining invariably without the sanctuary so that it might never be profaned.

In this interior society man finds wisdom and therewith the All—not the wisdom of this world, which is but scientific knowledge, which revolves round the outside but never touches the centre (wherein is contained all power), but true wisdom and men obedient thereto.

All disputes, all controversies, all the things belonging to the false prudence of this world, fruitless discussions, useless germs of opinion which spread the weeds of disunion, all error, schisms and systems are banished therefrom. Neither calumny nor scandal are known. Every man is honoured. Satire, that spirit which seeks diversion to the disadvantage of its neighbour, is unknown. Love alone reigns. Never does the monster of calumny rear among the sons of wisdom its serpent head; estimation in common prevails, and this only; the faults of a friend are passed over; there are no bitter reproaches heaped on imperfection. Generously and lovingly, the seeker is placed upon the way of truth. It is sought to persuade and touch the heart of those who err, leaving the punishment of sin to the Lords of Light.

Want and feebleness are protected; rejoicings are made at the elevation and dignity which man acquires. No one is raised above another by the fortune which is a gift of chance; he only counts himself most happy who has the opportunity to benefit his brethren; and all such men, united in the spirit of love and truth, constitute the Invisible Church, the society of the Kingdom within, under that one Chief who is God.

We must not, however, imagine that this society resembles any secret order, meeting at certain times, choosing its leaders and members, united by special objects. All associations, be these what they may, can but come after this interior illuminated circle, which society knows none of the formalities belonging to the outer rings, the work of man. In this kingdom of power the outward forms cease.

God Himself is the Power always present. The best man of his times, the chief himself, does not invariably know all the members, but the moment when it is the Will of God that they should be brought into communication he finds them unfailingly in the world and ready to work for the end in view.

This community has no outside barriers. He who may be chosen by God is as the first; he presents himself among the others without presumption, and he is received by them without jealousy.

If it be necessary that true members should meet together, they find and recognise each other with perfect certainty. No disguise can be used, neither hypocrisy nor dissimulation could hide the characteristic qualities of this society, because they are too genuine. All illusion is gone, and things appear in their true form.

No one member can choose another, unanimous choice is required. All men are called, the called may be chosen, if they become ripe for entrance.

Any one can look for the entrance, and any man who is within can teach another to seek for it; but only he who is ripe can arrive inside.

Unprepared men occasion disorder in a community, and disorder is not compatible with the

Sanctuary. This thrusts out all who are not homogeneous.

Worldly intelligence seeks this Sanctuary in vain; in vain also do the efforts of malice strive to penetrate these great mysteries; all is undecipherable to him who is not prepared; he can see nothing, read nothing in the interior.

He who is ripe is joined to the chain, perhaps often where he thought least likely, and at a point of which he knew nothing himself.

Seeking to become ripe should be the effort of him who loves wisdom.

But there are methods by which ripeness is attained, for in this holy communion is the primitive storehouse of the most ancient and original science of the human race, with the primitive mysteries also of all science. It is the unique and really illuminated community which is in possession of the key to all mystery, which knows the centre and source of nature and creation. It is a society which unites superior power to its own, and includes members from more than one world. It is the society whose members form a theocratic republic, which one day will be the Regent Mother of the whole World.

LETTER III

THE absolute truth lying in the centre of Mystery
is like the sun, it blinds ordinary sight and man sees
only the shadow. The eagle alone can gaze at the
dazzling light, and only the prepared soul can bear
the arcane lustre. Nevertheless, the great *Something*
which is the inmost of the Holy Mysteries has never
been hidden from the piercing gaze of him who can
bear the light.

God and nature have no mysteries for their
children. Mystery is caused by the weakness of
our own nature, unable to support light, because it is
not yet organised to bear the chaste sight of unveiled
truth.

This weakness is the Cloud that covers the
Sanctuary; it is the curtain which veils the Holy
of Holies.

But in order that man might recover the lost
light, strength and dignity, loving Divinity bent to
the weakness of its creatures, and wrote the truth
that is interior and eternal mystery on the *outside of
things*, so that man can transport himself through
this to their spirit.

These letters are the ceremonies or the externals of religion, which lead to the interior spirit—active and full of life—of union with God.

Among these letters there are also hieroglyphics of the Mysteries—the sketches and outlines of interior and holy truths which emblazon the curtain drawn before the Sanctuary.

Religion and the Mysteries go hand in hand to lead our brethren to truth; both have for object the reversing and renewing of our natures; both have for their end the re-building of a temple wherein Wisdom dwells with Love, or God with man.

But religion and the Mysteries would be useless phenomena if Divinity had not also accorded means to attain their great ends.

Now, these means have been always in the innermost sanctuary. The Mysteries are destined to build a temple to religion, and religion is required to unite Man with God.

Such is the greatness of religion, and such the exalted dignity of the Mysteries from all time.

It would be unjust to you, beloved brothers, that we should think that you have *never* regarded the Holy Mysteries in this *real* aspect, the one which shows them as the only means able to preserve in purity and integrity the doctrine of the important truths concerning God, nature and man. This doctrine was couched in holy symbolic language, and the truths which it contained, having been gradually translated among the outer circle into the ordinary languages of man, became in consequence more obscure and unintelligible.

The Mysteries, as you know, beloved brothers, promise things which are and which will remain always the heritage of but a small number of men; these are the secret things which can neither be taught nor sold publicly, which can be only acquired by a heart that has attained to wisdom and love.

He in whom this holy flame has been awakened lives in true happiness, content with everything, even in slavery, and in everything free. He sees the cause of human corruption and knows that it is inevitable. He hates no criminal, he pities him, he seeks to raise him who has fallen, and to lead back him who has strayed, because he feels, notwithstanding all the corruption, that in the *whole* there is no taint.

He sees with a clear eye the underlying truth in the foundation of all religion; he knows the sources of superstition and of incredulity—knows that they are *modifications* of truth, which has not attained perfect equilibrium.

We are assured, my esteemed brothers, that you consider the true Mystic from this aspect, and that you will not attribute to *his royal art*, that which the misdirected energy of some isolated individuals has made of this art.

It is, therefore, with these views, which accord exactly with ours, that you will compare religion, and the mysteries of the holy schools of Wisdom, to loving sisters who have watched, hand in hand, over the good of mankind since the necessity of our birth.

Religion divides itself into exterior and interior religion—exterior signifying ceremony, and interior the worship in spirit and in truth. The schools of wisdom are also within and without; the outer schools possessing the letter and the symbol, the inner reserving the spirit and meaning. External religion is united to the inner by ceremonies, and the outer schools of the mysteries are linked with the inner by symbol. Yet a little while, and the spirit will restore the living letter, the Cloud will be lifted from the Sanctuary, symbols will pass into vision and words into true understanding. He who reveres the Holy Mysteries will make himself understood no longer by speech and the outward sign, but by the spirit of language and the truth of signs.

Thus religion will be no longer an external ceremony, but hidden and holy mysteries will penetrate through symbol into the outer worship, to prepare men for the worship of God in spirit and in truth.

Very soon the night of symbol will disappear, the light will bring forth the day and the holy obscurity of mysteries no longer veiled will manifest in the splendour of full truth.

The ways of light are prepared for the elect, for all who can walk therein. The vestibule of nature, the temple of reason and the sanctuary of Revelation will form but one Temple. Thus the great edifice will be completed—that edifice which consists in the re-union of man with nature and God.

A perfect knowledge of man, of nature and of God will be the lights which will enable the leaders of humanity to bring back from every side their wandering brothers, those who are led by the prejudices of reason, by the turbulence of passion, to the ways of peace and knowledge. The crown of those who rule the world will be pure reason, their sceptre native love, and the Sanctuary will impart to them that unction, even that force, by which the minds of the people will be emancipated and their physical condition relieved.

We are approaching the period of light, and the reign of wisdom and love—that of God, Who is the source of light. Brothers of light, there is but one religion, whose simple truth spreads in all religions, as in branches, returning through multiplicity into the unity of the tree.

Sons of truth, there is but one order, but one Brotherhood, but one association of men who are agreed in the sole object of acquiring the light. From this centre misunderstanding has brought forth innumerable Orders, but all will return, from the multiplicity of opinions, to the only truth and to the true Order—the association of those who are able to receive the light, the *Community of the Elect.*

With this measure all religions and all orders of man must be measured. Multiplicity is in the ceremony of the exterior ; truth is but one in the interior.

The multiplication of fraternities is in the manifold interpretation of the symbols caused by the lapse of time, needs of the day, and other circumstances. The true Community of Light *can* be only one.

The exterior symbol is only the sheath which holds the inner ; it may change and multiply, but it can never weaken the truth of the interior ; moreover, the letter was necessary ; we ought to seek and try to decipher it—so to discover the interior sense.

All errors, divisions, all misunderstandings, all which in religions and in secret societies tends to divagation can only concern the letter—the outer veil of symbol, ceremony and rite. What rests behind remains always pure and holy.

Soon the time for those who seek the light will be accomplished, for the day comes when the old will be united to the new, the outer to the inner, the high with the low, the heart with the brain, man with God, and this epoch is destined for the present age. Do not ask, beloved brothers, why for the present age? Everything has its time with those who are limited by time and space. It is in such wise according to the unvarying law of the Wisdom of God, Who has co-ordinated all in harmony and perfection.

The elect should first labour to acquire both wisdom and love, in order to earn the gift of power, which unchangeable Divinity gives only to those who *know* and those who *love*.

Morning follows night, the sun rises, and all moves

on to full mid-day, where shadows disappear in the vertical splendour. ❧The letter of truth must exist in the first place ; then comes the practical explanation, then the truth itself ; and it is only thereafter that the Spirit of Truth can descend Which testifies to truth, and sets the seals closing the light. ❧He who can receive the truth will understand. It is to you, much-loved brothers, you who labour to reach truth, you who have so faithfully preserved the glyph of the holy mysteries in your temple, it is to you that the first ray of truth will be directed ; this ray will pierce through the cloud of mystery, and will announce the full day and the treasure which it brings.

Do not ask *who* those are who write to you ; look at the spirit, not the letter—the thing, not at persons. Neither pride, self-seeking, nor any unworthy motive can exist in our retreats ; we know the object and the destination of man, and the light which lights us works in all our actions.

We are especially called to write to you, dear brothers in the light ; and that which gives power to our commission is the truth which we possess, which also we will pass on to you at the least sign, and according to the measure of the capacity of each.

Light is apt for communication, where there is reception and capacity, but it constrains no one, and waits its reception tranquilly.

Our desire, our aim, our office is to revivify the dead letter and to spiritualise the symbols, turning the passive into the active and death into life ; but this we cannot do *by ourselves*, only through His spirit of light Who is Wisdom, Love and the Light of the world.

Until the present time the Inner Sanctuary has been separated from the Temple, and the Temple beset with those who belong only to the precincts; but the day is coming when the Innermost will be re-united with the Temple, in order that those who are in the Temple can influence those who are in the outer courts, so that the outer may pass in.

In our sanctuary all the hidden mysteries are preserved intact; they have never been profaned by the uninitiated or soiled by the impure.

This sanctuary is invisible, as is a force which is only known through its action.

By this short description, my dear brothers, you can tell who we are, and it will be superfluous to assure you that we do not belong to those restless natures who seek to build in this common life an ideal after their own fantastic imaginations. Neither do we belong to those who wish to play a great part in the world, and who promise miracles that they themselves do not understand. We do not represent either that class of malcontents who would like to take vengeance on certain ranks in life, who have no better object than the desire of dominating others, the passion for adventure and things extravagant.

We can also assure you that we belong to no sect or association save the one true and great company of all those who are able to receive the light. We do not confess to prejudgments, of what kind soever ; we are not of those who think it their right to mould all after their own model, who seek arrogantly to re-model all other societies ; we assure you faithfully that we know *exactly* the innermost of religion and of the Holy Mysteries ; that we possess with absolute certainty all that has been surmised to be in the Adytum ; and that this same possession gives us the strength to justify our commission, imparting to the dead letter and hieroglyphic everywhere both spirit and life.   The treasures in our sanctuary are many ; we understand the spirit and meaning of all symbols and all ceremony which have existed since the day of Creation to the present time, as well as the most interior truths of the Holy Books, with the laws which govern the rites practised by primitive peoples.

We possess a light by which we are anointed, and by means of which we read the hidden and secret things of nature.

We possess a fire which feeds us, which gives us the power to act upon everything in nature.   We possess *a key to open* the gate of mystery, and *a key to shut* nature's laboratory.   We know of a bond which will unite us to the Upper Worlds, and will reveal to us their sights and their sounds.   All the marvels of nature are subordinate to the power of our will, and this will is united with Divinity.

We have mastered the science which draws directly from nature, wherein there is no error, but there are truth and light only.

In our School we are instructed in all things, because our Master is the Light itself and its essence. The plenitude of our scholarship is the knowledge of the bond between the divine and spiritual worlds, between the spiritual world and the elementary, between the elementary, in fine, and the material world.

By these knowledges we are in condition to co-ordinate the spirits of nature and the heart of man.

Our science is the inheritance promised to the Elect—otherwise, to those who are duly prepared for receiving the light—and the practice of our science is the plenitude of Divine Alliance with the children of men.

We could often tell you, beloved brothers, of marvels relating to the hidden things in the treasury of the Sanctuary, and these would amaze and astonish you; we could speak to you about things from which the profoundest philosophy is as far removed as the earth from the sun, but to which we are near as the inmost light to Him who is innermost of all.

Only inward persuasion and thirst after the good of our brethren should actuate one who is capable of receiving light even from the source of light—at that source where the thirst for wisdom can be satiated and the hunger after love satisfied. Wisdom and love dwell in our retreats; the stimulus of their reality and of their truth is our magical power.

We assure you that our treasures, though of infinite value, are concealed in so simple a manner that they entirely baffle the researches of opinionated science;

these treasures would bring to carnal minds both madness and sorrow, but they are and they ever remain to us the pearls without price of the highest wisdom.

My best blessing upon you, O my brothers, if you understand these great truths. The recovery of *the triple word* and of its power will be your reward. Your happiness will be in helping to re-unite man with man, with nature and with God, which is the real work of every craftsman who has not *rejected the Corner Stone.*

Now we have fulfilled our trust ; we have announced the approach of high noon, and the joining of the inner Sanctuary with the Temple ; we leave the rest to your own free will.

We know well, to our bitter grief, that even as the Saviour was not understood in His personality, but was ridiculed and condemned in His humility, so also His Spirit, when it shall appear in glory, will be rejected and despised by many. Nevertheless the coming of His Spirit must be announced in the Temples, that it may be fulfilled, even as it is written : " I have knocked at your doors and you have not opened them to Me; I have called and you have not listened to My voice; I have invited you to the wedding, but you were busy with other things."

May Peace and the light of the Spirit be with you !

LETTER IV

As infinity in numbers loses itself in the unit which
is their basis, and as the innumerable rays of a circle
are united in a single centre, so it is also with the
Mysteries; their hieroglyphics and infinitude of
emblems have the object of exemplifying but one
single truth. He who knows this has found the key
to understand everything, and all at once.

There is but one God, but one truth, and one way
which leads to this grand Truth. There is but one
means of finding it.

He who has discovered this way possesses everything therein; all wisdom in one book alone, all
strength in one force, every beauty in a single object,
all riches in one treasure only, every happiness in one
perfect felicity. And the sum of all these perfections
is Jesus Christ, Who was crucified and Who rose again.
Now, this great fact, expressed thus, is, it is true,
only an object of faith, but it can become also one of
experimental knowledge, as soon as we are instructed
how Jesus Christ can be or become all this.

This great mystery was always an object of instruction *in the Secret School of the invisible and interior*

41

Church ; this great knowledge was understood in the earliest days of Christianity under the name of *Disciplina Arcani.* From this secret school are derived all the rites and ceremonies extant in the Outer Church. But the spirit of these grand and simple verities was withdrawn into the Interior, and in our time it is entirely lost as to the external.

It has been prophesied long ago, dear brothers, that all which is hidden shall be revealed in these latter days ; but it has also been predicted that many false prophets will arise, and the faithful are warned not to believe every spirit, but to prove them if they really come from God (1 John iv. *passim*). The apostle himself explains how this truth is ascertained. He says : " Hereby know ye the Spirit of God : every spirit which confesseth that Jesus Christ is come in the flesh is of God : and every spirit which confesseth not . . . is not of God." That is to say, the spirit who separates in Him the Divine and human *is not from God.*

We do—on our own part—confess that Jesus Christ is come in the flesh, and hence the Spirit of Truth speaks by us. But the mystery that Jesus Christ is come *in the flesh* is of wide extent and great depth, and in it is contained the knowledge of the divine-human, and it is this knowledge that we are choosing to-day as the object for our instruction.

Since we are not speaking to neophytes in matters of faith, it will be much easier for you, dear brothers, to conceive the sublime truths which we will present to you, as without doubt you have already chosen for the object of your holy meditation various preparatory subjects.

Religion considered scientifically is the doctrine of the conversion of man separated from God into man re-united with God. Hence its sole term is to unite every human being with God, through which union alone can humanity attain its highest felicity, both temporally and spiritually.

This doctrine, therefore, of *re-union* is of the most sublime importance, and being a doctrine it necessarily must have a method by which it leads us, firstly, to knowledge of the correct path of re-union, secondly, to instruction upon the correct means and how these should be suitably co-ordinated to the end.

This grand concept of re-union, on which all religious doctrine is concentrated, could never have been known to man *without* Revelation. It has always been outside the sphere of scientific knowledge, but this very ignorance of man has made Revelation absolutely necessary to us; otherwise we could, unassisted, have never found the means of rising out of our state of ignorance.

Revelation entails the necessity of faith therein, because he who has no experience or knowledge whatsoever of a thing must necessarily believe if he wishes to know and have experience. If faith fails, there is no desire for Revelation, and the mind of man closes, by itself, its own door and road for discovering the methods contained in Revelation only. As action and re-action follow each other in nature, so also inevitably Revelation and faith act and re-act. One cannot exist without the other, and the more faith a man has the more will Revelation be made to him of matters which lie in obscurity. It is true, and very true, that all the veiled truths of religions, even those veiled most deeply, those most difficult to us, will one day be justified before a tribunal of strictest reason; but the weakness of men and their lack of penetration in perceiving the relation and correspondence between physical and spiritual nature, require that the highest truths should only be imparted gradually. The holy obscurity of the mysteries is thus on account of our weakness, and the growing splendour of their light is graduated for the same reason— to strengthen that weakness till our eyes can bear its fulness. In every grade at which the believer in Revelation arrives, he obtains clearer light, and this progressive illumination becomes the more convincing, because every truth of faith so acquired is more and more vitalised, passing finally into conviction.

Hence faith is founded on our weakness and also on the full light of Revelation which will, in its communication with us, direct us—according to our capabilities—to the gradual understanding of things, so that in due order the cognisance of the most elevated truths will be ours.

Those objects which are quite unknown to human sense belong necessarily to the domain of faith. Man can only adore and be silent, but if he wishes to demonstrate matters which cannot be manifested objectively, he necessarily falls into error. Man should adore and be silent, therefore, until the time arrives when these objects in the domain of faith become clearer, and, therefore, more easily recognised. Everything proves itself by itself as soon as we have acquired the interior *experience* of the truths revealed through faith, so soon as we are led by faith to vision, or, in other words, to full cognisance.

In all time have there been men illuminated of God who had this interior knowledge of the things of faith demonstrated objectively, either in full or partly, according as the truths of faith passed into their understanding or their hearts. The first kind of vision—and this purely intellectual—was called *Divine illumination.* The second was entitled *Divine inspiration.* The inner sensorium was opened in many to divine and transcendental vision, which was called ecstasy when the sensorium was so enlarged that it entirely dominated the outer physical senses.

But this kind of man is always inexplicable, and such he must remain to the person of mere sense who has no organs receptive of the transcendental and supernatural. Nor must we be surprised that one who has drawn near to the world of soul should be counted as extravagant, and even a fool, for common judgment is restricted by the common horizon, and "the natural man receiveth not the things of the Spirit of God, for they are foolishness unto him and he cannot know them, because they are spiritually judged" (1 Cor. xi. 14)—*i.e.*, because his spiritual senses are not open to the transcendental world, so that he can have no more objective cognisance of such world than a blind man has of colour; thus the natural man has lost these interior senses, or rather, the capacity for their development is neglected almost to atrophy.

Thus also, mere physical man is, in general, spiritually blind, having his interior eye closed, and this again is one of the consequences of the Fall. Man then is doubly miserable; he not only has his eyes blindfolded to the sight of high truths, but his heart also languishes a prisoner in the bonds of flesh and blood, which confine him to animal and sensuous pleasures and deny those which are more elevated and genuine. Therefore are we slaves to concupiscence, to the domination of tyrannical passions; therefore do we drag ourselves as paralysed sufferers supported on crutches—the one crutch being the weakness of mere human reason, and the other sentiment—the one daily giving us appearance instead of reality, the other making us constantly choose evil, imagining it to be good. Of such is our woeful condition.

Men can only be happy when the bandage which intercepts the true light falls from their eyes, when

the fetters of slavery are loosened from their hearts.
The blind must see, the lame must walk, before
happiness can be understood. But the great and
all-powerful law to which the felicity of man is
indissolubly attached is the one following: "Man,
let reason rule over your passions!"

For ages has man striven to teach and to preach,
with, however, the result, after so many centuries,
of the blind leading the blind; for in all the foolishness of misery into which we have fallen, we do
not yet see that of ourselves we can effect nothing,
that man wants more than man to raise him from
this condition.

Prejudices and errors, crimes and vices, only
change from century to century; they are never
extirpated from humanity; reason without illumination flickers faintly in every age, in the heavy
air of spiritual darkness; the heart, exhausted with
passions, also remains the same.

There is but One who can heal these evils; but
One who is able to open our inner eyes, so that
we may behold Truth; but One who can free us
from the bonds of sensuality.

This One is Jesus Christ, the *Saviour of Man*,
the *Saviour* because He wishes to extricate us from
the consequences which follow the blindness of our
natural reason, or the errors arising from the passions
of ungoverned hearts.

Very few men, beloved brothers, have a true and
exact conception of the grand scheme which is

termed the Redemption of Man; many suppose
that Jesus Christ the Lord has only redeemed or
re-bought us by His Blood from *damnation, otherwise the eternal separation* of man from God; but
they do not believe that He could also deliver
those who are bound in Him and confide in Him
from the miseries of this earth-plane!

Jesus Christ is the Saviour of the World; He is
the deliverer from all human wretchedness; He has
redeemed us from death and sin. But how could
He be all this if the world must languish perpetually
in the night of ignorance and in the bonds of
passion? It has been clearly predicted in the
Prophets that the time of the Redemption of His
people, the first Sabbath of time, *will come.* Long
ago ought we to have acknowledged this most
consolatory promise; but the *want* of the true
knowledge of God, of man and of nature has been
the real hindrance which has ever obstructed our
sight of the great Mysteries of the faith.

You must know, my brothers, that there is a dual
nature, one pure, spiritual, immortal and indestructible, the other impure, material, mortal and destructible. Pure and indestructible nature preceded
that which, though pure, was destructible. This
latter originated solely through the disharmony and
disproportion of substances which form destructible
nature. Hence nothing is permanent until all dis-
proportions and dissonances are eradicated, so that
all remains in harmony.

The imperfect conception regarding spirit and matter is one of the principal causes which prevent many verities of faith from shining in their true lustre.

Spirit is a substance, an essence, an absolute reality. Hence its properties are indestructibility, uniformity, penetration, indivisibility and continuity. Matter is not a substance, it is *an aggregate*. Hence it is destructible, divisible and subject to change.

The metaphysical world is one *really existing*, perfectly pure and indestructible, whose Centre we call Jesus Christ, whose inhabitants are known by the names of Angels and Spirits.

The physical world is that of phenomena, and it possesses no absolute truth; all that we term truth is here but relative, the shadow and the phenomena only.

Our reason here borrows all its ideas from the senses; hence they are lifeless and dead. We draw everything from external objectivity, and our reason is like an ape who imitates what nature shows him outwardly. Thus the light of the senses is the principle of our earthly reason, sensuality the motive for our will, tending therefore to animal wants and their satisfaction. It is true, however, that we feel higher motives imperative, but up to the present we do not know either where to seek or where to find.

In this world, where everything is corruptible, it

is useless to look for a pure *principle* of reason
and morality or a motive for the Will. This must
be sought for in a more exalted world—where all
is pure and indestructible, where reigns a Being
all wisdom and all love—a Being that by the
light of His wisdom can become for us the true
principle of reason, and by the warmth of His
love the true principle of morality. Thus the
world neither can nor will become happy until
this Real Being is received by humanity in full
and has become its All in All.

Man, dear brothers, is composed of indestructible
and metaphysical substance, as well as of material
and destructible substance, but in such a manner
that the indestructible and eternal is, as it were,
imprisoned in the destructible matter.

Hence two contradictory natures are compre-
hended in the same man. The destructible substance enchains us to the sensible, the other seeks
to deliver us from these chains, and to raise us to
the spiritual. Hence again the incessant combat
between good and evil: for ever and absolutely
the good desires reason and morality, while the
evil tends daily towards error and passion.

The fundamental cause of human corruption is
to be found in the matter from which man is
formed. For this gross matter oppresses the action
of the transcendental and spiritual principle, and
is the true cause of blindness in our understanding
and errors in our inclinations.

The fragility of a china vessel results from the clay out of which it is formed. The most beautiful impression that clay of any sort is able to receive must always remain fragile because the matter of which it is composed is itself fragile. Thus do men remain likewise frail, notwithstanding all our external culture.

When we examine the causes of the obstacles keeping the natural man in such deep abasement, they are found in the grossness of the matter in which the spiritual part is, as it were, buried and bound.

The inflexibility of fibres, the immovability of temperaments, in those who wish to obey the refined stimulation of the spirit, are, as it were, the material chains which bind us, preventing in us the action of those sublime functions of which the spirit is capable.

The nerves and fluidity of the brain can only yield us rough and obscure notions derived from phenomena—not from truth and the things themselves; and as we cannot, by the strength of our thinking powers alone, have sufficient balance to oppose representations strong enough to counteract the violence of external sensation, the result is that we are governed by our passions, and the voice of reason which speaks softly internally is deafened by the tumultuous noise of the elements which keep our mechanism going.

It is true that reason strains to raise itself above

this uproar, and wishes to decide the combat, seeking to restore order by the light and force of its judgment. But its action is only like the rays of the sun constantly hidden by clouds.

The grossness of all the matter in which material man consists, with the tissue of the whole edifice of his nature, is the cause of that disinclination which holds the soul in continual imperfection.

The heaviness of our thinking power follows in general from its dependence upon gross and un-yielding matter, which forms the bonds of flesh, and is the true source of all error and vice. Reason, which should be an absolute legislator, is continually slave to sensuality, which raises itself as regent and, governing the reason that is drooping in chains, follows its own desires.

This truth has been felt for long, and it has always been taught that reason should be sole legislator. It should govern the will and never be governed itself.

Great and small feel this truth; but no sooner is it desired to put it in execution than the animal will vanquishes reason, and then the reason subjugates the animal will; thus in every man the victory and defeat are alternate, and this power and counter-power cause a perpetual oscillation between good and evil, or the true and the false.

If man wishes to be led to the true and the good in such manner that he shall act only in accordance with the laws of reason, and from the purified will, it is absolutely necessary to constitute the pure reason sovereign in man. But how can this be done when the matter out of which many men are formed is more or less brutal, divisible and corruptible, the source of that misery, illness, poverty, death, want, of those prejudices, errors and vices which are the necessary consequence of the limitation of an immortal spirit in the bonds of brute and corruptible matter. Sensuality is bound to rule if reason is fettered, and reason is fettered assuredly when the weak and unclean heart repels the pure light.

Yes, friends and brothers, such is the general fate of man, and as this state of things is propagated from man to man, it may in all justice be called the hereditary corruption of our race.

We observe, in general, that the powers of reason act upon the heart with reference to the specific constitution of the matter of which man is made. It is also extremely remarkable that the sun vivifies this animal matter according to the measure of its distance from the solar body, that it makes it as suitable to the functions of animal economy as to a degree more or less raised of spiritual influence. Diversity of nations, their peculiarities as a result of climate, the variety of character, passions, manners, prejudices and customs, even their virtues and their vices, depend entirely upon the specific constitution of the matter from which they are formed, and in which the imprisoned spirit operates accordingly. Man's capacity for culture is modified in conformity with this constitution, which even affects his science, for this can only modify people so far as there is matter present that is susceptible of such modification, and therein consists the capacity for culture suitable to such people, and dependent partly on climate, partly on descent.

Generally, we find the same kind of man weak and sensual everywhere, wise just in so far as his physical matter allows reason to triumph over the sensuous, or foolish as the sensuous obtains mastery over the more or less fettered spirit. In this lies the evil and the good specially belonging to each nation, as well as to each isolated individual. We find in the world at large the same corruption inherent in the matter from which man is made, only under various forms and modifications.

From the lowest animal condition of savage nature man enters into the social state, primarily through his wants and desires ; strength and cunning, the chief qualities of the animal, accompany him and develop into other forms.

The modifications of these fundamental animal tendencies are endless ; and the highest degree to which human culture, as acquired by the world, has attained up to the present has not carried things further than the putting of a finer polish on the substance of our animal instincts. This means to say that we are raised from the rank of the brute to that of the refined animal.

But this period was necessary, because on its accomplishment begins a new era, when the animal instincts being fully developed, there commences the evolution of more elevated desires, working towards light and reason.

Jesus Christ has written in our hearts in exceedingly beautiful words this great truth, that man must seek in his common clay for the cause of all his sorrows. When He said, "The best man, he who strives the most to arrive at truth, sins seven times a day," He intended to show that in a man of the finest organisation, the seven powers of the spirit are still so closed that the seven sensuous actions overcome him daily after their respective fashions.

Thus the best man is exposed to error and passions; the best man is weak and sinful; the best man is not a free man, and, therefore, exempt from pain and trouble; the best man is subject to sickness and death, because these things are the inevitable consequences incidental to the corrupt matter of which he is formed.

It follows, therefore, that there can be no hope of higher happiness for humanity so long as the corruptible or material forms the principal substantial part of our being. The impossibility of mankind to transport itself, of itself, to true perfection, is a despairing thought, but, at the same time, one full of consolation, because, in consequence of this radical impossibility, a more exalted and perfect being than

man permitted himself to be clothed in this mortal
and destructible envelope *in order* to make the mortal
immortal, and the destructible indestructible; herein
is to be sought the true reason for the Incarnation of
Jesus Christ.

Jesus Christ, or the Anointed of the Light, is the
splendour of God, the wisdom which came forth from
God, the Son of God, the substantial Word by which
all is made, and which existed from the beginning.
Jesus Christ, the Wisdom of God working in everything, was as the centre of Paradise and the world of
light.   He was the only real organism by which
Divine power could be communicated, and this
organism is the immortal and pure nature, that indestructible substance which gives new life and raises
all things to happiness and perfection.   This pure
incorruptible substance is *the pure element* in which
spiritual man lived.

From this perfect element, which God only in-
habited, from this substance out of which the first
man was formed, that man was separated in the Fall.
By partaking of the Tree of Good and Evil, the good
and incorruptible principle combined with the bad
and corruptible one, and man was self-poisoned, so
that his immortal essence retreated interiorly, and
the mortal, pressing forward, clothed him externally.
Thus disappeared immortality, happiness and life,
mortality and death being the results of the change.

Many men cannot understand the idea of the Tree
of Good and Evil; this tree was, however, the pro-

duct of movable but central matter, in which destructibility had somewhat the superiority over the indestructible principle. The premature use of its fruit was that which poisoned Adam, robbing him of his immortality and enveloping him in material and mortal clay. In this manner he fell a prey to the Elements *which originally he governed.* This unhappy event was, however, the reason why Immortal Wisdom, the pure metaphysical element, clothed itself with a mortal body and was voluntarily sacrificed, so that its Interior Powers could penetrate into the centre of the destruction, and could thus raise gradually all that which is mortal into the immortal state.

When it came about quite naturally that immortal man became subject to mortality through the enjoyment of mortal fruit, it happened, also quite naturally, that mortal man could only recover his former dignity through the enjoyment of Immortal Matter.

All passes naturally and simply under God's Reign, but in order to understand this simplicity it is requisite to have pure ideas of God, of nature and of man. And if the sublimest Truths of faith are still, for us, wrapped in impenetrable obscurity, the reason is that we have up to this present severed the connection between God, nature and man.

Jesus Christ spoke to His most intimate friends when He was still on this earth, of the grand mystery of Regeneration, but all that He said seemed obscure, and they could not then receive it ; the development of the great Truths was reserved for these latter days, as the greatest and the last Mystery of Religion, wherein all Mysteries return, as into Unity.

Regeneration is no other than a dissolution of, and a release from, this impure and corruptible matter, which enchains our immortal essence, plunging into deathly sleep its obstructed vital force. There must be necessarily a real method to eradicate this poisonous ferment, which breeds so much suffering for us, and thereby to liberate the obstructed vitality.

There is, however, no other means to find this excepting by religion, for religion, looked at scientifically, is the doctrine which proclaims re-union with God, and it must of necessity show us how to arrive thereat. Are not Jesus and His living knowledge the principal object of the Bible and the centre of all desires, hopes and efforts of Christians? Have we not received from our Lord and Master, while still He walked with His disciples, the profoundest solutions of the most hidden truths? When He was with them in His glorified Body after the resurrection, did He not give them a higher revelation with regard to His Person, and lead them still more deeply into central knowledge of truth?

Will He not realise that which He said in His Sacerdotal Prayer, St. John xvii. 22, 23: "And the glory which thou hast given to Me I have given unto them, that they may be one, even as We are One: I in them, and they in Me, that they may be perfected into one."

As the disciples of the Lord could not comprehend this great mystery of the new and last alliance, Jesus Christ transmitted it to the latter days, to that future now arriving. This alliance is called the Union of Peace. It is then that the law of God will be engraven in the heart of our hearts ; we shall all know the Lord ; we shall be His people, and He will be our God.

All is prepared for this actual possession of God, this union really possible here below ; and the holy element, the efficacious medicine for humanity, is revealed by God's Spirit. The table of the Lord is ready and every one is invited ; the "true bread of Angels" is prepared—as it is written : "Thou didst give them Bread from Heaven."

The holiness and the greatness of the Mystery which contains within itself every mystery here obliges us to be silent, except in respect of its effects.

The corruptible and destructible are destroyed, and replaced by the incorruptible and by the indestructible. The inner sensorium opens and links us on to the spiritual world. We are enlightened by wisdom, led by truth, nourished with the torch of love. Unimagined strength develops in us wherewith to vanquish the world, the flesh and the devil. Our whole being is renewed and made suitable for the actual dwelling-place of the Spirit of God. Command over nature, intercourse with the upper worlds, the delight of visible intercourse with the Lord—these are granted also!

The hoodwink of ignorance falls from our eyes; the bonds of sensuality break; we rejoice in the liberty of God's children.

We have told you the chiefest and most important fact; if your heart, having the thirst for truth, has laid hold on the pure ideas that you have gathered from all this, and has received in its entirety the grandeur and the blessedness of the thing itself as object of desire, we will tell you further.

May the Glory of the Lord and the renewing of your whole nature be meanwhile the highest of your hopes!

LETTER V

In our last letter, my dear brothers, you granted me your earnest attention to that highest of mysteries, *the real possession of God ;* it is therefore necessary to give you fuller light on this subject.

Man, as we know, is unhappy in this world because he is made out of destructible matter that is subject to trouble and sorrow.

His fragile envelope—*i.e.,* the body—exposes him to the violence of the elements—to pain, poverty, suffering, illness. These are his normal fate while his immortal spirit languishes in the bonds of sense. Man is unhappy, because he is ill in body and soul, and he possesses no true medicine either for soul or body.¹

Those whose duty it is to govern and lead other men to happiness, are as other men, also weak and subject to the same passions and prejudices.

Therefore, what fate can humanity expect ? Must the greater part of it be always unfortunate ? Is there no salvation for all ?

Brothers, if humanity as a whole is ever capable of being raised to a condition of true happiness, such state can only be possible under the following conditions :—

Firstly, poverty, pain, illness and sorrow must become much less frequent.   Secondly, passions, prejudice and ignorance must diminish.

Is this at all possible with the nature of man, when experience proves that, from century to century, suffering only assumes fresh form ; that passions, prejudices and errors always cause the same evils ; and when we realise that these things only change shape, that man in every age remains much the same weak man?

There is a terrible judgment pronounced upon the human race, and this judgment is that men can never become happy so long as they will not become wise ; but they will never become wise while sensuality governs reason, while the spirit languishes in the bonds of flesh and blood.

Where is the man that has no passions ?   Let him show himself.   Do we not all wear the chains of sensuality more or less heavily?   Are we not all slaves, all sinners ?

This realisation of our low estate excites in us the desire for redemption ; we lift up our eyes on high, and an angel's voice says—*the sorrows of man shall be comforted.*

Man being sick in body and soul, this mortal sickness must have a cause, and *this cause* is to be found in the very matter out of which he is made.

The destructible imprisons the indestructible ; the light of wisdom is imprisoned in the deeps of obscurity ; the *ferment of sin* is in us ; in this ferment human corruption originates, and its propagation continues therein, with all the consequences of original sin.

The healing of humanity is only possible through the destruction of this ferment of sin ; hence we have need of a physician and a true remedy. But one invalid cannot be cured by another ; the man of destructible matter cannot re-make himself of indestructible matter ; dead matter cannot awake what is dead ; the blind cannot lead the blind.

Only the Perfect can bring anything to perfection ; only the Indestructible can raise the destructible to its own state ; only the Living can wake the dead.

This Physician and this active Medicine cannot be found in death and destruction—only in superior nature, where all is perfection and life !

It is ignorance of the harmony between Divinity and nature, between nature and man, which is the true cause of all prejudice and error. Theologians, philosophers, moralists, all wish to regulate the world, and they fill it with endless contradictions. Theologians do not see the accordance of God with nature and fall therefore into error. Modern philosophers study only matter, not the connection of pure nature with Divine Nature, and therefore announce the falsest opinions. Moralists will not recognise the inherent corruption of human nature, and they expect to cure by words, when means are absolutely necessary.

Thus the world, man and God, ever continue in dissension; one opinion drives out another; superstition and incredulity take turn about in dominating society, separating man from the word of truth when he has so much need of approaching her.

It is only in the true Schools of Wisdom that one can know God, nature and man; in these, for thousands of years, work has been done in silence to attain the highest degree of this knowledge,—the union of man with pure nature and with God.

This great end, God and nature, towards which everything moves, has been represented to man symbolically in every religion; all the symbols and holy glyphs are but the letter by which man can, step by step, recover the highest of all mysteries, divine, natural and human, or otherwise learn the means of healing his unhappy condition, and of the union of his being with pure nature and with God.

We have attained this epoch under God's guidance. Divinity, remembering its covenant with man, has provided the means of cure, the means of man's restoration to his original dignity, of his union with God, the Source of his happiness.

The knowledge of this method is the science of Saints and of the Elect; its possession is the inheritance promised to God's children.

Now, my beloved brothers, I want you to grant

me your most earnest attention to what I am about
to say.

*In our blood there is lying concealed a slimy matter
(called the gluten) which has a nearer kinship to
animal than to spiritual man. This gluten is the
body of sin.*

It is matter which can be modified in various
manners, according to the stimulus of sense; and
according to the kind of modification and change
occurring therein, so also vary the divers sinful
tendencies of man.

In its most violent expansion this matter produces
pride; in its utmost contraction, avarice, self-will
and selfishness; in its repulsion, rage and anger;
in its circular movements, levity and incontinence;
in its eccentricity, greediness and drunkenness; in
its concentricity, envy; in its essence, sloth.

This ferment of sin, as original sin, is more or less
working in the blood of every man; it is transmitted from father to son, and in its perpetual propagation everlastingly hinders the simultaneous action
of spirit with matter.

It is quite true that man by his will-power can
put limits to the action of this body of sin, and can
dominate it so that it becomes less active, but to
destroy and annihilate it altogether is beyond his
power. Here then is the cause of the combat which
we are constantly waging between the evil and the
good in us.

This body of sin forms the ties of flesh and blood

6

which, on the one side, bind us to our immortal spirit, and, on the other, to the tendencies of the animal man.   It is, as it were, the allurements of the animal passions that smoulder and take fire at last.

The violent reaction of this body of sin in us, or sensuous stimulation, is the reason why we choose, for the want of calm and tranquil judgment, rather the evil than the good, because the active fermentation of this matter impedes the quiet action of the spirit necessary to instruct and sustain the reason.

This same evil matter is also the cause of our ignorance, because, as its thick and inflexible substance surcharges the fine brain-fibres, it prevents the co-action of reason, which is required to penetrate the objects of the understanding.

Thus falseness and all evils are the properties of this sinful matter, this body of sin, just as the good and the true are essential qualities of the spiritual principle within us.

By a thorough understanding of this body of sin we can learn to see that we are beings morally ill, that we have need of a physician with a medicine which will destroy and eradicate the evil matter always fermenting banefully within us, a remedy that will restore us to moral health.

We learn also to recognise clearly that all mere moralizing with words is of little use *when real means are necessary.*

We have been moralizing in varied terms for centuries, but the world remains pretty much the same. A doctor would do little good in talking only of his remedies, it is necessary for him actually to prescribe his medicines; he has, however, first to see the real state of the sick person.

The condition of humanity—the moral sickness of man—is a true case of poisoning, consequent upon the eating of the fruit of that tree in which corruptible matter predominated.

The first effect of this poison resulted thus: the incorruptible principle, the body of life, as opposed to the body of sin or death, whose expansion caused the perfection of Adam, concentrated itself inwardly, and the external part was abandoned to the government of the elements. Hence a mortal matter gradually covered the immortal essence, and the loss of this central light was the cause subsequently of all man's sufferings.

Communication with the world of light was intercepted, the interior eye—which had the power of seeing truth *objectively*—was closed, and the physical eye opened to the plane of changing phenomena.

Man lost all true happiness, and in this deplorable condition he would have forfeited the means of restoration to health, were it not that the love and mercy of God, Who had no other object in creation than the greatest happiness for its creatures, afforded a means of recovery. In this means, man, with all his posterity, had the right to trust, in order that, while still in his state of banishment, he might support his misfortune with humility and resignation, finding in his pilgrimage, moreover, the great consolation that all his corruptible parts could be restored perfectly through the love of a Saviour.

Despair would have been the fate of man without such revelation.

Man, before the Fall, was the living Temple of Divinity, and at the time when this Temple was destroyed, the plan to rebuild it was already projected by the Wisdom of God. At this period begin the Holy Mysteries of every religion, which are all and each in themselves, after a thousand varying modes, according to time and circumstances, and method of conception by different nations, but symbols repeated and modified of one solitary truth, and this unique truth is—*regeneration, or the re-union of man with God.*

Before the Fall man was wise, he was united to Wisdom ; after the Fall he was no longer one therewith ; hence a true science, through express Revelation, became absolutely necessary to restore the union.

The first Revelation was as follows :—

The state of immortality consists in the immortal permeating the mortal. Immortal substance is Divine Substance, and is no other than the magnificence of the Almighty throughout nature, the substance of the world and spirits, the infinity, in short, of God, in whom all things move and have their being.

It is an immutable law that no creature can be

truly happy when separated from the source of happiness. This source is the magnificence of God Himself.

By partaking of destructible nourishment, man himself became destructible and material ; matter, therefore, as it were, places itself between God and man ; that is to say, man is not directly penetrated and permeated by Divinity, and, in consequence, he is subject to the laws regulating matter.

The divine in man, imprisoned by the bonds of this matter, is his immortal part, the part that should be at liberty, in order that its development should again rule the mortal. Then once more would man regain his original greatness.

But a means for his cure, or a method to externalize what is now hidden and concealed within, is requisite. Fallen and unwise man, of himself, can neither know nor grasp this expedient ; he cannot even recognise it, because he has lost pure knowledge and the light of true wisdom ; he cannot take hold of it, because the remedy is infolded in interior nature, and he has neither the strength nor power to unlock this hidden force.

Hence Revelation, in order to learn this means and have strength to acquire this power, is necessary to man.

The necessity for the salvation of man was the cause of the determination of Wisdom, or the Son of God, to give Himself to be known by man, *being the pure substance out of which* all has been made.

In this pure substance power is reserved to vivify dead substance, and to purify all that is impure.

But before that could be done, before the inmost part of man, the divine in him, could be once more penetrated and re-opened, and the whole world be regenerated, it was requisite that this Divine Substance should incarnate in humanity, should become human, and transmit the Divine and Regenerative Force to humanity; it was necessary also that this Divine-Human Form should be slain, in order that the divine and incorruptible substance contained in His blood should penetrate into the recesses of the earth, and thenceforth work a gradual dissolution of corruptible matter, so that in due time a pure and regenerated earth may be restored to man, the Tree of Life again planted therein, that by partaking of its fruit, containing the true immortal essence, mortality in us may be once more annihilated, and man healed by the fruit of the Tree of Life, just as he was once poisoned by partaking of the fruit of death.

This constitutes the first and most important revelation on which all others are founded, and it has been carefully preserved from mouth to mouth among the chosen of God up to this time.

Human nature required a Saviour; this Saviour was Jesus Christ, the Wisdom of God itself, reality from God. He put on the envelope of humanity, to communicate anew to the world the divine and immortal substance, which was nothing else but Himself.

He offered Himself voluntarily, in order that the *pure essential force* in His blood could penetrate directly, bringing with it the potentiality of all perfection to the hidden recesses of the earth.

Himself, both as High Priest and as Victim at the same time, entered into the Holy of Holies, and after having accomplished all that was necessary, He laid the foundation of the Royal Priesthood of His . Elect, and taught these through the knowledge of His person and of His powers after what manner they should lead, as the first born of the spirit, other men, their brethren, to universal happiness.

And here begin the Sacerdotal Mysteries of the Elect and of the Inner Church.

The Royal and Priestly Science is that of Re-generation, or the science of the reunion of fallen man with God. It is called *Royal Science*, because it leads man to power and the dominion over nature. It is called Sacerdotal, because it sanctifies and brings all to perfection, spreading grace and bene-diction everywhere.

This Science owes its immediate origin to the *verbal revelation* of God; it was always the Science of the Inner Church of Prophets and of Saints; and it recognised no other High Priest but Jesus Christ, the Lord.

This Science has a triple object: firstly, the re-generation of the individual and isolated man, or the first fruits of the Elect; secondly, of many men; thirdly, of all humanity. Its exercise consists in the highest perfecting of oneself and of everything in nature.

This Science was never taught otherwise than by the Holy Spirit of God, and by those who were in unison with this Spirit; it is beyond all other sciences, because it can alone teach the knowledge of God, of nature, and of man in a perfect harmony; other sciences do not understand truly either God or nature, either man or his destination. It enables man to distinguish the nature which is pure and incorruptible from that which is corruptible and impure, and by the separation of the latter to attain the former. In a word, the subject-matters of this Science are the knowledge of God in man, of Divinity in nature; these being, as it were, the Divine impression or seal, by which our inner selves can be opened and can arrive at union with Divinity.

Thus re-union was the most exalted aim, and hence the Priesthood derived its name, *religio, clerus regenerans.*

Melchizedek was the first Priest-King; all true Priests of God and of nature descend from him, and Jesus Christ Himself was united with him as priest after the order of Melchizedek. This word is literally of the highest and widest significance —מלכיצדק (MLKIZ-DQ). It means literally instruction in the true substance of life and in the separation of this true vital substance from the mortal envelope which encloses it.

A priest is one who separates that which is pure nature from that which is impure nature, the substance which contains all from the destructible matter which occasions pain and misery. The sacrifice or that which has been separated consists in bread and wine.

 Bread means literally the substance which contains all; wine the substance which vitalises everything.

Therefore, a priest after the order of Melchizedek is one who knows how to separate the all-embracing and vitalising substance from impure matter, one who knows how to employ it as a real means of reconciliation and re-union for fallen humanity, in order to communicate to man his true and royal privilege of power over nature, and the Sacerdotal dignity, or the ability to unite himself by grace to the upper worlds.

In these few words is contained the mystery of God's Priesthood, and the occupation and aim of the Priest.

But this royal Priesthood was only able to reach perfect maturity when Jesus Christ Himself as High Priest had fulfilled the greatest of all sacrifices, and had entered into the Inmost Sanctuary.

We are here on the threshold of new and great mysteries which are worthy of your most earnest attention.

When, according to the wisdom and justice of God, it was resolved to save the fallen human race, the Wisdom of God had to choose the method which afforded in every aspect the most efficacious means for the consummation of this great object.

When, after the enjoyment of a corruptible fruit—which permeated him with the ferment of death—man was poisoned so thoroughly that all around him became also subject to death and destruction, then Divine mercy was constrained to establish a counter remedy, which could be taken after the same manner; it contained within itself the divine and revitalising substance, so that by receiving this immortal food, poisoned and death-stricken man could be healed and rescued from his suffering. But in order that this Tree of Life could be replanted here below, it was requisite beyond all things that the corruptible material in the centre of the earth should be first regenerated, resolved and made capable of being again one day a universally vitalising substance.

This capacity for new life, bringing about the dissolution of corruptible essence which is inherent in the centre of the earth, was only possible in so far as Divine Vital Substance assumed flesh and blood to transmit the hidden forces of life to dead nature. This was done through the death of Jesus Christ. *The tinctural force* which flowed from His blood penetrated to the innermost parts of the earth, raised the dead, rent the rocks and caused the total eclipse of the sun by driving from the centre of the earth, wherein the light penetrated, the central darkness to the circumference, and therein laying the foundation of the future glorification of the world.

Since the death of Jesus Christ, the divine force, driven to the earth's centre by the shedding of His blood, works and ferments perpetually to press outward, and to fit and prepare all substances gradually for the great cataclysm which is destined to take place in the world.

But the rebuilding of the world's edifice in general was not the only aim of Redemption. Man was the principal object in the shedding of Christ's blood; to procure for him, even in this material sphere, the highest possible perfection by the amelioration of his being, Jesus Christ submitted to infinite suffering.

He is the Saviour of the world and of man. The object or cause of His Incarnation was to rescue us from sin, misery and death.

Jesus Christ has delivered us from all evil by His flesh, which He sacrificed, and by His blood, which He shed for us.

In the clear understanding of this *flesh* and this *blood* of Jesus Christ lies the true and pure knowledge of the real regeneration of man.

The mystery of union with Jesus Christ, not only spiritually *but also corporeally*, is the greatest aim of the Inner Church. To become one with Him in spirit and in being is the fulfilment and plenitude of all efforts of the Elect.

The means for this real possession of God are

hidden from the wise of this world, and revealed to the simplicity of children.

Do thou, O vain philosopher, bend down before the grand and Divine Mysteries which thou canst not understand in thy wisdom, and for the penetration of whose secrets the feeble light of human reason, darkened by sense, can give thee no measure!

LETTER VI

Whoa!

GOD became man to deify man. Heaven united itself with earth to transform earth into Heaven.

But in order that these divine transformations can take place, an entire change, a complete and absolute overturning and upsetting of our being, is necessary.

This change, this upsetting, is called re-birth. *To be born*, simply means to enter into a world in which the senses dominate, in which wisdom and love languish in the bonds of individuality.

To be *re-born* means to return to a world where the spirit of wisdom and love governs, where animal-man obeys.

The re-birth is triple; there is, firstly, the re-birth of our intelligence; secondly, of our heart and our will; and, finally, the re-birth of our entire being.

The first and second kinds are called the spiritual, and the third the corporeal re-birth.

Many pious men, seekers after God, have been regenerated in the mind and will, but few have known the corporeal re-birth. Those to whom it has been given have only received it that they might serve as *agents* of God, in accordance with great objects and high intentions, and to bring humanity nearer to felicity.

It is now necessary, my dear brothers, to lay before you the true order of re-birth. God, Who is all strength, wisdom and love, works eternally in order and in harmony.

He who will not receive the spiritual life, he who is not born anew from the Lord, cannot enter into heaven.

Man is engendered through his parents in original sin, that is to say, he enters into the natural life and not the spiritual.

The spiritual life consists in loving God above everything and your neighbour as yourself. In this twofold love consists the *principle* of the new life.

Man is begotten in evil, in the love of himself and the things of this world. Love of himself! Self interest! Self gratification! Such are the substantial properties of evil. The good is in the love of God and the neighbour, in knowing no other love but that of mankind, no interest but that affecting every man, no other pleasure but the well-being of all.

It is by such sentiments that the spirit of the children of God is distinguished from the spirit of the children of this world.

To change the spirit of this world into the spirit of the children of God is to be regenerated, and this means to put off the old man and to clothe one's self with the new.

But no person can be re-born if he does not know and put in practice the following principles—that truth is the object of faith and the good that of our activity as well as our abstinence from action. Therefore, he who desires to be re-born ought first to know what belongs to re-birth. He ought to understand, meditate and reflect on all this. Afterwards he should act according to his knowledge, and the result will be a new life.

Now, as it is first necessary to know, and to be instructed in all that appertains to re-birth, a doctor, or an instructor, is required, and if we know one, faith in him is also necessary, because of what use is a teacher if his pupil have no confidence in him?

Hence, the commencement of re-birth is faith in Revelation.

The disciple should begin by believing that the Lord, the Son, is the Wisdom of God; that He is from all Eternity from God; and that He came into the world to bring happiness to humanity. He should believe that the Lord has full power in heaven and on earth, and that all faith and love, all the true and the good come from Him alone; that He is the Mediator, the Saviour and Governor of men.

When this most exalting faith has taken root in us, we shall think often of the Saviour; our thoughts, turned towards Him, will unfold from within; and by His grace reacting in us, the seven closed and spiritual powers are opened.

The way to happiness.—Do you wish, man and brother, to acquire the highest happiness possible? Search for truth, wisdom and love. But you will not find these except in unity, and this is the Lord Jesus Christ, the Anointed of God.

Seek, then, Jesus Christ with all your strength; seek Him from the fulness of your heart.

The beginning of the heart's elevation is in the knowledge of its emptiness, and from this knowledge there originates the need of a higher power to seek Him, wherein is the beginning of faith.

Faith gives confidence, but faith has also its order of progress. First comes historic faith, then moral, then divine, and finally *living* faith. The progression is as follows : Historical faith begins when we recognise—by history and revelation—that a man existed who was called Jesus of Nazareth; that he was a man set apart from men by his extraordinary love of humanity, the good which he conferred thereon, and the life which he led; that—in a word—he was the best of men and one who demands not only all our attention but all our love. From this simple historical faith in the *existence* of Jesus will evolve moral faith, and the development of this consists in the acquirement of virtue by its search and practice, so that we see and find real pleasure in all that is taught by this Man; we find that His simple doctrine is full of wisdom and His teaching full of love; that His intentions towards humanity are straight and true, and that He willingly suffered death for the

sake of justice. Thus, faith in His Person will be
followed by faith in His Divinity.

This same Jesus Christ tells us now that He is Son
of God ; He emphasizes His words by His miracles,
His own resurrection, and thereafter by instructing
His disciples in the highest mysteries of nature and
religion.

Here natural and reasonable faith changes into
divine faith, and we begin to believe that the Christ
was God made man. From this faith it results that
we hold as true all that we do not yet understand,
but which He tells us to believe. Through this faith
in the Divinity of Jesus, by entire surrender to Him,
and by faithful attention to His laws, there is at last
produced that living faith, by which we find *within
ourselves*, as something that is true in *our own experience*, all that we have believed in hitherto merely with
the confidence of a child ; and this living faith, proved
by experience, is the highest grade of all.

When our hearts, through living faith, have received
Jesus Christ, then this Light of the World is born
within us as in a humble stable.

Everything in us is impure, surrounded by the
spider-webs of vanity, covered with the mire of
sensibility.

Our will is the Ox that is under the yoke of its
passions. Our reason is the Ass which is bound
through the obstinacy of its opinions, its prejudices,
its follies.

In this miserable and ruined hut, the home of all

the animal passions, can Jesus Christ be born in us through faith.

The simplicity of our souls is as the shepherds who brought their first offerings, until at last the three principal powers of our royal dignity, our reason, our will, and our activity [1] prostrate themselves before Him and offer Him the gifts of truth, wisdom and love.

Little by little the stable of our hearts changes itself into an exterior Temple, where Jesus Christ teaches, but this Temple is still full of Scribes and Pharisees.

Those who sell doves and the money changers are still to be found therein ; these must be driven out, and the Temple changed into a House of Prayer.

Little by little Jesus Christ chooses all the good powers in us to announce Him. He heals our blindness, purifies our leprosy, raises the dead powers into living forces within us ; He is crucified in us, He dies, and He is gloriously raised again as Conqueror within us. Afterwards His personality lives in us, and instructs us in exalted mysteries, until He has made us complete and ready for the perfect Regeneration—when He mounts to heaven and thence sends us the Spirit of Truth.

But before such a Spirit can act in us we experience certain changes. The seven powers of our understanding are lifted up within us, but afterwards the seven powers of our heart or of our

[1] The Three Magi.

will, and this exaltation takes place in the following manner. The human understanding is divided into seven powers; the first is that of looking at objects outside ourselves—*intuitus*. By the second we perceive the objects so regarded—*apperceptio*. By the third, that which has been perceived is reflected upon—*reflexio*. The fourth is that of considering these objects in their diversity—*fantasia, imaginatio*. The fifth is that of deciding upon something—*judicium*. The sixth co-ordinates all these according to their relationships—*ratio*. The seventh and last is the power of realising the whole intellectual intuition—*intellectus*.

This last contains, so to say, the sum of all the others.

The will of man divides itself similarly into seven powers, which, taken together as an unit, form the will of man, being, as it were, its *substantial* parts.

The first is the capacity of desiring things apart from oneself—*desiderium*. The second is the power to annex mentally things desired for oneself—*appetitus*. The third is the power of giving them form, realising them so as to satisfy desire—*concupiscentia*. The fourth is that of receiving inclinations, without deciding upon acting upon any, as in the condition of passion—*passio*. The fifth is the capacity for deciding for or against a thing, liberty—*libertas*. The sixth is that of choice or resolution actually taken—*electio*. The seventh is the power of giving the object chosen an existence—*voluntas*. This seventh power also contains all the others in one figure.

Now the seven powers of the understanding, like the seven powers of our heart and will, can be ennobled and exalted in a very special manner, when we embrace Jesus Christ, as being the wisdom of God, for the principle of our reason, and His whole life, which was all love, for motive power of our will.

Our understanding is formed after that of Jesus Christ: (1) When we have Him in view in everything, so that He becomes the only motive point of all our actions—*intuitus;* (2) when we perceive His actions, His sentiments and His spirit everywhere—*apperceptio;* (3) when in all our thoughts we reflect upon His sayings, and think in everything as He would have thought—*reflexio;* (4) when we so shape our course that His thoughts and His wisdom are the only object for the exercise of our imagination—*fantasia;* (5) when we reject all thoughts which are not in conformity with His, and choose those only to which He might also confess—*judicium;* (6) when, in short, we co-ordinate the whole edifice of our ideas and spirit upon the model of His ideas and spirit—*ratio;* (7) when, as the result of these, there is born in us a new and more brilliant light, surpassing far the light of reason and of the senses—*intellectus.* Our heart is also reformed in like manner, when in everything: (1) We lean on Him only—*desiderare;* (2) we wish for Him only—*appetere;* (3) we desire only Him—*concupiscere;* (4) we love Him only—

amare ; (5) we choose only that which He is, and we avoid all that He is not—*eligere ;* (6) we live only in harmony with Him, after His commandments, institutions and orders—*subordinare ;* whereby (7) there is born a complete union of our will with His, so that we abide in Jesus Christ as one sense, one heart ; so that the new man is little by little born in us ; so that Divine Wisdom and Love unite to form in us the new spiritual man, in whose heart faith passes into sight, in comparison with which living faith the treasures of India can be considered but as ashes.

This actual possession of God or Jesus Christ in us is the term towards which all the mysteries converge, like radii to the centre of a circle ; the highest of religious mysteries is in this consummation.

The Kingdom of God is a kingdom of truth, morality and happiness. It operates in the saints from innermost to outermost side, and spreads itself· gradually by the Spirit of Jesus Christ into all nations, to institute everywhere an Order by means of which the individual can profit as well as the race —by which our human nature can be raised to its highest perfection, and sick humanity can be cured of all the evils of its weakness.

Thus the love and spirit of God will one day alone vivify all humanity ; they will awake and rekindle the powers of the race, will lead it to the goals of Wisdom and place it in suitable relationships.

Peace, fidelity, domestic harmony, love between

nations, will be the first fruits of this Spirit. In-spiration of good without false similitudes, the exaltation of our souls without too severe a tension, beneficent warmth in the heart without turbulent impatience, will approach, reconcile and unite all the various parts of the human race, long separated and divided by many differences, and stirred up against each other by prejudices and errors.   So in one Grand Temple of Nature, great and little, poor and rich, will all sing the praise of the Father of Love.

NOTES BY THE TRANSLATOR

NOTE TO LETTER I

I AM afraid that some readers who are interested in "Mysticism," or rather are desirous of entering into its study, may be deterred from doing so by reading these letters of the excellent Mystic, Eckartshausen. The reason is that his doctrine of Regeneration has been so much misunderstood owing to an over-familiarity with the ordinary signification of that deeply important word which modern Religion mostly gives us. Nevertheless, no reader can fail to see that Eckartshausen has a very real and vital reason for all that he says.

His language is extraordinarily simple, so much so that many may consider that he hides deeper matter purposely.

This is not quite the case; in all Catholic and central truth there are, though not opposing, various meanings, each opening, as it were, according to the grade of the student's own spiritual understanding.

Indeed, it is very frequently urged against mystic and alchemic writings that they purposely and selfishly veil the truth. No doubt in many cases it has been done purposely, but for sincerely good reasons which inquiry would amply endorse. Still it is by no means a true bill against "mystic" writings that the language is deliberately symbolic, allegoric, or in a sort of cipher-code, as it were, in which one word is mischievously meant for another and so forth. I have heard all alchemic works described, indeed once thought so myself, as a farrago of pure bosh. But we know, as most people nowadays who pretend to any philosophy at all, that there are other planes of nature besides the physical, and that mystic and alchemic writings are *not* generally dealing with physical or mental matters and nomenclature. They refer to higher planes of nature—and if a student be able to enter into higher planes, the terms and expressions take their simple and rightful place. But all that a student can do in his first study of these matters is to try and discern somewhat where the planes change, where the writer means literally on the higher plane and parabolically on the physical or on what plane is the literalness? But most alchemic writing is hyperphysical. Origen says "to the literal-minded (or carnal) we teach the Gospel in the historic or literal way, but to the proficients, fired with the love of Divine Wisdom, we impart the Logos." Also we must remember that these writers were spiritual giants—men who had gone through the vital process of Regeneration, and who wrote to others in like condition, not to the carnal-minded or literal men, who have their spiritual "sensorium," as Eckartshausen calls it, still sealed.

We are, therefore, grateful when a spiritual giant like Eckartshausen writes as he does in simpler fashion—one more suitable to the plane of intellectuality on which we usually are. He tells us literally that man has fallen from his high estate, as we have all been taught in "common" Christianity, and he proceeds to point out the spiritual rationale whereby man may attain his former greatness. In doing so, he explains in a most suggestive manner the real value of the rites and ceremonies of Catholic Christendom, the Church, as he teaches, being the outer manifestation of that Inner Society (the nameless one), that Society of the Elect which has always existed, and must still exist, for the protection of mankind. If this Sacred Circle, this Celestial Church, did not *sub*sist, our earthly sinful Churches could not *ex*ist. That they *do* is a proof of its holy Guardianship, and Eckartshausen's letters on the subject, explanatory of this position, are most instructive. There are doubtless a few elect souls who are so richly laden with the ten talents which they have earned in preceding lives, that they can, so to say, take the Kingdom of Heaven with violence and obtain their Regeneration and Immortality early in this life, without possibly belonging to any Society, whether Church organisation or otherwise, but to most people this is impossible ; and we then, as humbler students, do well to give heed to the great

importance of Christian rites and ceremonies—especially that of the Sacred Supper.   This is, of course,
not new teaching to instructed Christians, but I would
respectfully suggest that Eckartshausen *does* lead the
understanding to higher ground and higher possibili-
ties, as an authorised Initiate, than Church teaching
can do, because Catholic Doctrine does not and *cannot*
explain fully.   It is the function of the Church only
to enunciate *ex cathedra* as the legitimately appointed
external channel of communication ; but certain
writers, Initiates and Regenerate men, have special
offices as instructors and explainers.   Therefore those
people who have not the gift of Faith to receive
enunciated Doctrine, have indeed much to be thank-
ful for in that there are such writers who *are* permitted to explain *the reason why* of doctrine and
dogma.   To minds, then, who are not gifted with
Faith, or who have not attained to it, the writings of
the mystics are priceless, as no doubt through them
the student who only commenced the quest from
mere but honest curiosity and desire, if, however, he
continue sincere and earnest, can without doubt rise
not only to the region of faith, but in addition with a
clear understanding, and he then is in a still better
condition for further advancement.   Mad is that
person who with the grace and gift of Faith to
commence with has left his talent untouched !

The Cloud upon the Sanctuary is written in
six letters, and they show the meaning of Revelation, the means whereby man can receive it, the

supreme importance of man's Regeneration and the means whereby he can attain to it. And I may here say that a Regenerated Man in Mystic phraseology is equivalent to "Mahatma," or may be more; in modern theosophic terms, it means a Master, and until man attains to this rank he is not able fully to recognise *the* Master, so must always remain until that time outside the Temple, not yet fit to enter within the sacred precincts and be hailed as a true Builder by the Master-Builder Himself. Regeneration is moreover the only means by which he gains freedom from Karma, and is thenceforth freed from the Circle of Necessity or Re-birth. There is one other matter to note, both in reading sacred writ and mystic writers, that if we find one meaning pretty clear throughout we may conclude we *have* one key, but that is all, and the fact that we understand this side of the truth is just the reason that we have not *all* the truth. If we have this well in our minds it will be a useful check upon spiritual pride, for it will keep us always respectful to our brothers' and sisters' versions of the matter. Nevertheless there is something so real, so solid, so concrete in the presentment of Mystic Truth that if the foundation be firmly realised it is remarkable how much more easily the building is raised than we could imagine while wandering in the phantasmal regions of astral revelations—that realm of chaos out of and from which man has been lifted, by being created Rational Man, but towards which he too easily returns on a retrograde course. We must also note that Eckartshausen lived and wrote at the period of the French Revolution—at an era very similar to our own in all but its sad consummation. "Magic" was the fashion, and quite as much was known then on these matters as is known now. There were spiritual circles, occult societies, brotherhoods, and a great searching into the "hidden things of the Spirit."

We have Saint-Martin's valuable authority at that period for thinking very highly of Eckartshausen as a man who worked and thought centrally, and whose writings commanded his highest respect.

NOTE TO LETTER II

There is an expression in the fourth paragraph which is puzzling. The literal translation would of course be "many worlds." The same word is also used in the last paragraph: " It counts its members from more than one world." I am at a loss to give the real meaning. Translating it as society, circle, set of people, would at once give it a sense of limitation ; but it probably may mean other worlds—*i.e.*, planes or planets.

There is a paragraph in Carpenter's work, *From Adam's Peak to Elephanta*, which I must here mention ; he says, *à propos* of the rites and ceremonies of a Hindu Temple : " The theory is that all

the ceremonies have inner and mystic meanings—
which meanings in due time are declared to those
who are fit—and that thus the temple, institutions
and ceremonies constitute a great ladder by which
men can rise at last to those inner truths which lie
beyond all formulas and are contained in no creed."

This is exactly the argument of Eckartshausen,
with the exception of the last phrase, as, *au contraire*,
he would say that creeds are quite different to
formulas—creeds being the synthetic enunciation of
verities, so shorn of all but the absolutely necessary
words that no one but masters of theology can at
all correctly enlarge them. However, the interesting
point is the similar view of the importance of the
outer ceremony on the part of the Hindu priests.
It would be insulting the understandings of my
readers if I were to point out the obvious fact that
though Eckartshausen speaks so constantly of the
Church rites and ceremonies he is *not* alluding to
any special Church. In the next letter, which is
an extremely interesting one, the word Temple is
substituted for Church. A Church properly speaking means a body of worshippers. A Temple means
a building containing a shrine. This distinction is
of importance. In France the R.C. Church calls
the Protestant places of worship Temples, which
according to its views they cannot be, as it would
not consider that the Protestants have the Sacred
Vessels or offices, or anything really pertaining to
a shrine.

Nevertheless, it is also clear that Eckartshausen speaks with so much respect of rites and ceremonies, symbols and hieroglyphics, which he may regard as otherwise than necessarily Egyptian, of course, that one feels that he must have thought with more respect of those Churches that have kept a larger amount of rite and ceremony than those which deliberately docked them. These latter emulated too soon the exalted condition of being beyond all formula, and so fell below it, the tendency of mankind in a natural condition being towards outer manifestation. This, of course, is but a preliminary stage, but a long way ahead of the condition of not feeling any desire for such manifestation.

In speaking of the " Elect " we cannot be sufficiently careful not to fall into any error of thought on this matter by being influenced by any dregs of Calvinistic limitation. We cannot exalt our ideas on the subject high enough, for in fact we do not know anything at all about *who* and *what* are the Elect. Our Mystic is certainly not writing on ordinary lines, neither to ordinary people. One may be inclined, therefore, to say, "Oh, then it does not concern us!" But it does, for we never know when we may turn from the ordinary into the extra-ordinary. All that we have to do is—our best. We certainly shall be in the right if we exalt all theology, especially as conveyed through mystic writers (who seem to have the power of exalting the gold into still purer sublimation), as high as our imagination will go. The *possibility* of reaching this region will always be open to us, if we do not fall into the snare of imagining that we can easily experimentally arrive at such an altitude. All the letters of Eckartshausen point to a region of thought and action quite beyond recognised theology. We therefore infer that he and other mystics give us some of the information known to the inner Sanctuary, and not taught generally in the outer circles, that is, in the Churches of Christendom. We must certainly read the words " Christian Mysteries " between the lines. If we said that they mean the Sacraments, especially the Holy Supper, we should limit these mysteries to those that are acknowledged as such and given generally to Christian Europe. We must all of us see an advanced grade beyond the one which we can achieve, a grade of high initiation which will open these mysteries to us, an attitude of thought which at least must command our respect, and which certainly, if faithfully maintained, would in itself do much to advance us. The *fear* of God is the beginning of Wisdom, which, as Eckartshausen points out, is something *truly* comprehensive.

NOTE TO LETTER III

It appears to me most necessary that we should bear in mind, while reading the above, that as a rule mystic writing is, so to speak, synthetic. This seems a contradiction somewhat to the continual repetition of very similar words and ideas. It is, however, synthetic in this respect, that though apparently diffuse, it is in reality condensed to the utmost.

There can be no manner of doubt that the author of these letters is addressing readers and hearers who are already advanced in philosophy. It is well now and then to use words in their true meaning, and in this instance to say that his hearers and readers must have been lovers of wisdom in the best sense, or he could not address them as he does. As I ventured to suggest in the note to the first letter, Regeneration to the mystic does not mean the degenerate interpretation of modern theology.

The *royal art* hinted at in these letters is well called *royal*, as it is neither more nor less than a faithful following, under the inspiration of God's wisdom, of the Creative power itself, or rather the re-creation of man back to his original royal standpoint. What other work can compare to this?

No wonder that theology in the early ages meant something very different in sense of fulness to the emptiness of theology as expounded in modern times! This indeed does hold the original letter, but the mysteries lying behind it wait now for the true priest to decipher.

The Royal Art may be taken as pertaining to the Christian Mysteries which Eckartshausen speaks of with such deep respect and reverence as being in the Inner Sanctuary. In that Inner Sanctuary, where we may surmise none but the elect or the re-created could enter! No wonder again that the prayers of such men ascended with sweet savour to the Master, no wonder that the work of such men was *efficacious* as from century to century they worked on in order and knowledge towards the great Consummation, when the end was achieved and the Temple in its perfection manifested as the "first Fruits," so that all who were ready saw, and all who were ready heard, for the day of the Gentiles had arrived.

Eckartshausen is, therefore, addressing the modern descendants in his day of those elect men—men who, coming after the Consummation, could never achieve again the same work, but who had entered into the Mysteries, and whose duty was to protect and cherish them. To all followers, however remote they may have been in his day, and in our days, from the special elect at the great period of the Church, there is the same work given.

Our author's synthetic language is really addressed, therefore, to minds already in possession of a vast quantity of knowledge, to whom it was not necessary to do more than point the discourse by short, direct, condensed description, for it is clear that, except in inculcating respect to the service of religion, there is little that would be directly teaching to an ordinary theological student, who, we will suppose, reads his exhortation with no knowledge of *what* interior process really meant. Indeed, it would seem to such rather assumption and assertion, especially the latter part, where Eckartshausen, speaking in the plural, directly affirms his transcendental position, with no explanation as to the how and why.

It is, therefore, again clear that he is addressing real students of the Mysteries, and that his language will be sufficiently illuminative to those who are in the fortunate position of responding to this description. If they were empty and inflated claims, it is certain that his letters would long ago have been repudiated as worthless ; but we know that the opposite has been the case, and that no contradictions on his *own grounds* have ever been made.

One must notice, also, that in this letter, after speaking chiefly of the Church in the previous letters, it is the Temple that is generally referred to. It all seems to point to a conclusion, with which, I fancy, all students of these matters will agree, that the Church, whether Eastern or Western, is meant as the Receptacle for the letter, the enunciator of the synthesised unchangeable doctrine ; that its religion lies in symbol and glyph ; whereas it is reserved for another order, that of the Temple or the *redeemed men within the Church*, to hold the mystery therein concealed, forming the Nameless Society which is made up from chosen (*i.e.*, capable) men and women, out of the inner societies which have always existed as circles within, more and more nearly approaching the Sacred Centre. All mystics exhort students to respect and revere the religion in which they are born, being, as Eckartshausen so repeatedly points out, the standpoint from which the more interior journey can alone be made safely. The word mystery is often most annoying to some minds, as is also the continual holding out of apparently vague and illusive hopes and expectations. Eckartshausen especially says that he does not wish to awaken curiosity; but it is clear that he does awaken it. To some minds it will remain mere curiosity, but others will be stimulated to prolonged and patient search. There can be no doubt in such case that the road will open unexpectedly, and work will be pointed out that was not foreseen. Mystery not only means veiled knowledge, but also what is beyond our senses, so we call it mystery rightly, in opposition to exact science, which we know is within the capability of all industrious students, whereas mystery opens the possibility of undreamt of knowledge, and undreamt of happiness. By all the noble souls who, as we presume, have a right to say so, it is called the Pearl without price. The great philosophy of the East in its grand and sonorous language bears the same testimony, and we find that this jewel was ever the one quest of the first philosophers, to whom we are wisely once more directing earnest attention.

NOTE TO LETTER IV

It is of course evident that Eckartshausen is addressing two orders of mind—the reference to the Christian mysteries implying this.

It is, therefore, as well to follow his advice and be silent, lest *opinion* might not only be useless, but misleading. It is abundantly clear, however, with regard to Faith, the cultivation of which he urges, that he cannot mean the lower Faith which does so much duty for the greater gift. He cannot mean that Faith which fails to discern what is mere current opinion and superstition, a vast quantity of which pertinaciously clings round all religions. By Faith Eckartshausen means (I infer) an agreement with the great primal doctrines which he characterises as beyond the solution of reason, though this is NOT to be discarded in consequence, since he urges zealously the necessity of reason. It is abundantly clear, therefore, that Eckartshausen is advocating the cause, not of a blind superstition, as many people now imagine this religion of his to be, but of the highly philosophical, profoundly reasoned, and self-demonstrating system of Theosophy experimentally understood by the higher minds of more advanced grade, yet to others still a matter of faith, that is, of future knowledge, if the proper means for acquiring it are duly followed.

NOTE TO LETTER V

I am well aware that many readers of this fifth letter will think that the mystic who writes them was but a half-instructed philosopher, and that had he known the Bibles of other nations he would never have taught what will seem to them bigoted and sectarian doctrines. But before such dictum be recorded, is it not as well to remember that Eckartshausen and other mystics of his school especially say that all religions in their various manners confess to *the same object?* Eckartshausen in no case suggests the condemnation of any one among all the various religions; he seems to respect *all*, for he says that their aim and object is indifferently the Regeneration of Man. The stumbling-block and difficulty to most students, certainly to those who are students only of the neo-Buddhism of the present day, is the re-introduction of what is considered by such as exploded and narrow ideas, such as the need of man for Salvation, his inability to help himself, and the Redemption of man by the Sacrifice of the Jewish Saviour. It is not in my province or power to enter with ability into this discussion, but I would respectfully suggest these two things—firstly, are we quite sure, as Buddhist students, that we do understand the true hidden teaching of the Way of Salvation as known to Eastern Initiates; secondly, do we all understand it in Christianity itself? It is true, exoteric Buddhism, even when called esoteric, repudiates such doctrines, while the Christianity which admits them has taught them in such fashion that a large proportion of people born under Christianity repudiate them also. It is clear that the outer schools all repudiate them, and so it would seem that the Mystic Initiates preach doctrine no longer agreeable to our "sense of justice."

It is thought by many that the doctrines of Karma and Re-incarnation are much more satisfactory than Christian doctrines. Perhaps so, as modern Christianity is understood. But is evil Karma aught else but original sin in its *works* and *consequences?*

All knowledge is requisite, and it matters not so much how to attain knowledge, so that we do get it; therefore we owe a great debt of gratitude to the Eastern school for proving, from another aspect, the truth of our own, and one must recognise the great value of the recovery of these two doctrines. But I take my stand upon the ground that knowledge even of true doctrine is not always *directly* helpful. Indeed, as one most respected thinker says, "the doctrine of Karmic re-incarnation is in truth a terrible one in point of FACT, and hopeless for the individual." Again, therefore: What else is Karma but original sin and the consequence entailed on destructible matter? But this is a long subject and must not now be entered into, as it is equally unwise and useless to profane great subjects by inaccurate statement and mere polemics. Unhappily, owing to much vaporous and non-experimental discourse on the mysteries of Regeneration, more particularly the result of the Calvinist school, there was no doubt much profanation; and the reaction of many thoughtful and earnest minds, even from the very words, is due to the inner terror which they felt, though they did not understand, at this profanation.

The mystics put to us the great question: Can

man work out his own salvation? They say, No. The Eastern school, as we know it, which is not in its entirety, says Yes. It appears to me that the mere observation of life and society in the West says also, No. This may not apply to others.

The "Raj-yog" may be a perfect means of "salvation" to some nations. Is it to ours?

With regard to the text quoted in the last letter— "For a just man falleth seven times, and riseth up again"—it is referable to Proverbs xxiv. 16. The number seven is important.

We must bear in mind throughout these letters, just as in the Bhagavat Ghita, that two orders of minds are addressed. But the latter scripture, being a Sacred Book from *Catholic* source, has likewise universal as well as particular application, whereas mystics write as a rule particularly, though to the Initiate as well as the Postulant.

Note to Letter VI

I can but fear that, especially in this latter part, our noble teacher Eckartshausen may displease, even repel some of his readers. To the natural man the things of God are foolishness, and the intellect that is only equipped with the opinions of the twentieth century will probably feel even resentment at what may seem a suggested surrender of its whole nature in an ignoble manner, and that to follow out teachings savouring of the Roman

Catholic or Anglican Church, or even the Meeting House—as the ending suggests. Such a course will appear quite unsuitable to the intellectual, religious student of to-day. It is to these objections, which one feels come rather from the head than the heart, that I would like respectfully to suggest a few thoughts.

In the first place, Eckartshausen is addressing himself to the Elect, these last also including all who desire to know the things of the Spirit. Many are called but few chosen, for many have the desires but not the steadiness of purpose to carry them through; now Eckartshausen does not speak to these directly, but to the steady and determined student, and he leads these up to a point which we all feel that few can attain; this sense then of resentment is not altogether blameable, because it proceeds from an intuition of our own shortcomings and of the magnitude of the whole Work. In very simple words, the author puts before us the achievement by the individual man of the greatest Work— THE MAGNUM OPUS—that can be done on earth— the Conscious Possession of God. It is a work known and taught by the Eastern as all other true Schools; it is that of the entrance of finite mortal man into Omniscience, Immortality and Infinity. If we have, by too common use of such phrases, lowered and profaned our own ideals, it does not alter *the fact* that this possibility, as the hope of mankind, is of all things the most superb. Neither, because we feel as ordinary men and women that these things are too high for us, and our souls faint within us at the bare notion of such achievement, need we despair.

We must reflect that the whole purpose of Creation is for the ultimate full Manifestation of God in Man; that though we, as mere individuals, can make but small headway, we belong to humanity; that it is humanity which is to be restored to its pristine glory, not *as* God, but as fit vehicle for His glory to manifest. In aid of this there was consummated the superlative work of Christ's Incarnation as *a first fruits*—and Man, the greatest of God's works, this Catholic soul of man when Regenerate, brings about the great Redemption.

Yet few individuals have attained, or can attain, save those holy Priests of the Mysteries, those Saints, those Masters of the Rosy Cross, those just men *made perfect*, who lead the Way for us, they following the Leader of them all, the Master of Masters, Christ Jesus. We only follow as we can, remembering to our everlasting comfort that our feet are now already planted in the Kingdom, our faces are set Homeward, and our Faith supports us, so that we hold on, as it were, by the Fringe of His Garments, and are thus in the Fold of the Shepherd. Faith IS of the *substance* of things hoped for, and so our Faith is a proof of the substance to which we are annexed.

As to the objection that there are no such masters

and doctors now,—are there not? God does NOT
leave the World, neither any one, without them.
The Righteous man never dies. Every one of us,
according to our merit and grade, has a teacher of
some sort. Doubtless very few have arrived at the
point when what is called occult knowledge, or
spiritual philosophy, is either given or required; but
when any mind is able to learn intelligently and
rationally the important things of the Spirit, it does
not matter in what outward religion he may at first
be placed, for the Doctor and Master will surely
come at the right moment.

In these days there is an unfortunate misunderstanding afloat that information as to the things
of the Spirit means mainly knowledge concerning
psychical gifts, such as clairvoyance, clairaudience,
&c. Certainly there is very much to learn about
these serious matters that can only be studied
successfully in special manners, under authorized
teachers, who understand experimentally what they
teach. But most students are impelled by vanity
or shallow curiosity, and do not even intend to take
the real trouble that well-ordered Work entails.
These will not find—otherwise than that which they
seek. They will find but emptiness, like unto
apparitions created by the passions of their own
souls, having no substance, therefore not signifying
anything true, and yet that which they will not have
the Knowledge to understand. The *vaporous estate*
of Universal Being, as under the Satyric form of

" Pan," will conceal all truth, and they run the risk of going *astray* from *the Kingdom*.

To readers of Intellect who are dissuaded from the idea of the " Quest," as if it were derogatory to their intellect to have faith in that of which they know nothing, I would venture to suggest that the plan be tried, for nowhere does Eckartshausen, *or any other true* Mystic, imply that the intellect is to be stultified. On the contrary, it is asserted that the objects are so great and noble, that the intellect naturally, when really honourable to itself, humbles itself because of the nobility of that which is contemplated. In everything the Intellect, the *Rational* Soul, is regarded with respect as the proper vehicle wherewith to work, and it is only humbled by the Comparison which it makes when it sees the vast horizons dawning, when it leaves the small personal issues of the sense-life for the great and Catholic issues of the new life of Man. All this is not mere words ; it is meant precisely as said, not as a figment of the imagination which has no true root in itself, but as the recorded experience of the Wise Ones— which we simple ones would do well to respect.

In fine, with reference to these letters of Eckartshausen, it has been well advised that we should not place too gross an interpretation on the word *gluten* in connection with original sin. The same term has been used by other experienced Mystics to denote the sensuous spirit in the blood, our invisible animism, in fact, which, being consciously converted to its rational Principle, is thereby perceived to be devious and in need of reduction and rectification. This does not mean that the body of sin, "the wicked man," should die absolutely, but that he should repent and live righteously, henceforth becoming a body co-ordinate with the measure of the Divine Image, by which also he is thus re-capitulated into a new whole sensorium or principal One Sense.

Thus Dante, amongst others, in the *Paradiso*, speaks of the *Double* garment, the spiritual body and the glorified earthly body ; and Isaiah, also, lxi. 7 : "Therefore their Land shall possess the *double* and everlasting joy shall be unto them." Hence it is that the greatest and humblest of all earthly creatures, viz., the re-created pure Humanity, has been honoured by such as have correspondentially recognised the Handmaid of the Lord, the Servant-Form not yet glorified, which He vouchsafed to take upon Him, Who is our Catholic Example and means of Salvation.

And thus while the Angels, being divine Emanations, will be seen in the same aspect, after as before the final Crisis, the Souls of the Saints will bear a twofold garment ; the spiritual and the transmuted Sensorial Body fitly prepared and ready to be incorporated into a royal manifestation and ultimated Kingdom of God in Christ.

It may be observed that Mystics uniformly respect the historic tradition in a secondary sense, as if it were a husk for the safe keeping of the invaluable Kernel. So Dean Colet, in his Introduction to the Hierarchies of Dionysius, quoting him, says : " We have heard as a mystery that Jesus Christ was made in substance as a Man, but we know not *how* He was fashioned of the Virgin's Substance by a law other than natural, nor how with feet bearing a corporeal mass and weight of matter He passed dry shod over this watery and fleeting existence." Dionysius then goes on to say that these topics have been elsewhere set forth, referring apparently to treatises now lost. In any case, it is affirmed that neither in what he writes himself, nor in the mystical extract which he proceeds to quote from his Preceptor Hierotheus, is there anything explicit on the subject of the Incarnation and Redemption of Mankind.

A clear knowledge of this *how* has not been deemed essential to Salvation.

The method of Divine Works, and their recognizances or bonds of record, have been held inviolate by such as have entered into them from time to time; while a right faith is inculcated above all things, since Truth alone can veritably enter into Truth, in such wise as to constitute Itself simply in the apperception. "Blessed are they who have not seen and yet have believed"— that is to say, by an identical and willing insight, which is " the true Light which lighteth every man that cometh into the World."

Again : " The Church of God, which is situated

on a hill above the World in pure air and bright atmosphere, has supplied to it also, from the Vale of this world's misery, the material of its own felicity. For the Church by its lower portion, which is masculine and active, lifts upwards the higher and more passive portion of the world— much as the rays of the Sun refine and rarefy, by their heat, the surface portions of water—and so raise them on high that from it first it may fashion for itself a body. The external body, though coarser and more corporeal than the spiritual part of the Church, is yet more spiritual than the mundane as a whole.

"From this body in turn, and more material part of the Church, when sound and healthy, I mean," (continues the same writer) "from the highest and clearest quarter of it (*i.e.*, of the Ethereal sense), and from among such as have now almost become Spiritual, who are, as it were, the pure, clear and more vital blood of the Church ; from among such men, I say, in the passive portion of the Church, the most advanced are drawn into a spiritual state, that they may at length be active portions and spirits, but at first only purifying spirits whose whole duty and office consists in the purification and renewal and support of the humbler and more material (or sordid sensorial) portion of the Church.

"For between it, and God, and the Soul of the Church, come spiritual men, as the agents and workers of all. Just as in man, between his soul and his body, there intervene pure, subtle, bright, and fiery spirits, generated from the heat of the heart and the subtler blood; so in like manner, between God and the Church of assembled men, are some of the assembled men themselves from the clearer portion of the Church and its diviner blood, so to speak; spiritual men begotten of the warmth and love of God, who are midway between God and the rest of mankind depending on God through them, each according to his degree.

"The first in order which are nearer to the carnal portion of the Church quicken the flesh by their purifying virtue washing away men's sinful mortal nature, that they may live by hope in God. The second, who spiritualise the senses, illumine those who are purified and hoping in God; that with faith they may have a perfect *sense* of the Sacraments of the Church and every sacred Symbol and rejoice therein with the fullest belief. The third and highest are those who are intent upon God with all their affections and have a clear understanding of the simple *meaning* of each sense. These take such as have by faith had a sense of the symbols and sacraments; and as many of them as come to them in a fit and ripe state they make Contemplators of the simple meanings of the mysteries and Objects of religious faith according to their capacity, in order that what they have long had sense of under priests, they may now, under the Bishop, understand with the most perfect Love;

and being filled with the Mysteries, so far as they are capable, may be made perfect. *For light is an ethereal and unsubstantial thing unless it be intensified as it were with heat,* and the sight of sensible things is well-nigh empty and vain unless men be filled with a love of the Mysteries that are made intelligible.

" By the vision of the Mysteries, by love, and worship all things are completed and perfected, therefore the highest ones who perfect are the Bishops, the intermediate who illumine are the Priests, the lowest who purify are the Deacons. Those who are purified so as to have a single hope in God that they may stay themselves on Him consciously and in hope, may now breathe in Him, and being born again by *a new creation* may now become an entirely new creature. And thus does the whole system of the Church by purification, illumination and discipline in Christ, labour for man's steadfast simplicity and wise order and perfect goodness after the glorious pattern of the Angels, so that above the chaos and confusion of the World there may arise a bright array of simple and perfect men in God like a city set upon a hill, the light of the World and the salt of the Earth ; such as may shine beneath Christ their Sun with faith, hope and charity, and may illumine and give light to the world. But alas ! (as the same early teacher goes on to say) thick fumes and noisome blackness have now for a long while been exhaling upwards in such dense volume from the vale of benighted men, as well-nigh to overwhelm the light of that city ; so that Churchmen now shrouded in darkness, not knowing whither they go, have foolishly blended and confounded themselves with all ; so that again in the World there is nothing more confused and chaotic than the mass of men from amongst whom the seal of Christ, which He stamped upon it, has been almost effaced and destroyed by the promiscuous jostling of mankind in the universal disorder " (see Colet on the " Hierarchies," page 126).

The Cloud is upon the Sanctuary still; after so many centuries of faith, alternating with perplexity and doubt, it is becoming more dense perhaps; the darkness deepens even until it is felt. "A German Essayist on Dionysius" (Augustus Meyer) is probably right in saying that Mysticism chiefly springs up and flourishes when the established forms of religion have begun to lose their hold on men; when the instinctive longing of the Soul after the immortal and divine remains, but can find nothing to satisfy its cravings in the external rites of a failing Church.

From the hard and arid system of Peter Lombard, says Milman, the profound devotion of the middle ages took refuge in Mysticism, thereby following Aristotle's advice to enfeebled governments, that at decadent crises—in order to regain vigour—they should return to the principles on which they were originally founded.

Now the first philosophers taught that the Root-Principles of religion are concealed behind the Sacramental Mystery of Existence itself; into the nucleus of this it is therefore necessary to re-enter in order to recover them; and therefore sacred traditions have been provided as guides and incentives for the needs of such times as call for recuperation.

All holy scriptures have been regarded formerly by theosophic Doctors and by Kabalists of repute as remains of and witnesses to the spiritual life and psychic achievement of an Epoch that still stood in the full light of a primeval revelation. If they are unintelligible now it is because the conditions which produced them are supplied no longer. The Keys and Commentaries of subsequent Masters of Assemblies remain obscure also and even unintelligible, except in certain rare instances where individuals or elect communities have been momently involutionised towards a partial recognition of the Whole that is in all.

It has nevertheless been admitted by faithful students, even in these days, that the mystical interpretation of Scripture formerly by its more experienced Masters (as proved by their literary remains) came of no play of mere poetic fancy, no arbitrary readings into vulgar history of a meaning which it did not contain. It rested rather (as maintained one of the orthodox leaders of Church thought in a Bampton Lecture of 1895) on the

Principle that has been recognised by the faithful, that all sacred Utterances of spiritually circumstanced events are direct revelations of a Law that is eternal, and may accordingly be regarded as representative at each subsequent operation of that Law. The crises or judgments thereof in its vivid operative procedure are concomitant, while metaphysically separate from one another, as are the logical processes of this our common life in relation to vulgar knowledge. Thoughts travelling in logical sequence translate themselves at their conclusive crises into signs and forms of speech; so the Supernal Canons, in their infallible order, unfolding by and from the Divine Utterance, are a veritable Formal Syntax, as it were Angelic voicings, messengers of the one Law implied. Further developing down and deepening in complexity, scope and multiplicity as time rolls on, the same Eternal Mandate—increasing in figurative convertibility to the common understanding—becomes representable to the common soul, which being herself an Outcome and Image, as Plato says, delights in Images, and especially in such as belong to the exhibition and magnification of her own Prototype, from which Nature, having fallen off with the Fall of Man, fails to supply any adequate means towards the renovation of her Whole.

Here comes in the Church, with ritual, creed, discipline and dogma supernally derived, to remind, resuscitate and actuate, to warn, sustain and feed the latent Evidence, keeping the way of the Divine

Word open, apart from which the entrusted Talent wastes *now and afterward.*

" There are some," observes a learned writer, " who say there is no other Christ-soul than the higher Ego in Man ; as well say that there is no magnetic current but that which is in the needle of each compass. The Higher Self of every man manifest to that man himself and to all who can perceive in him the workings of the Higher, manifested in the Lower principles, the nature of the general guiding spirit or Over Soul of Humanity, the former being a micro-cosmic exhibition of the latter, which again is itself a manifestation of the cosmic Over Soul or Higher Self of the Universe, just as the great magnetic currents sweep from the Equator to the Pole, and the tiny magnetised needle makes the direction of the current manifest in a particular place and time. This ani-mating spirit then, whose purpose is re-union of Humanity with its Higher Self, has characteristics or attributes on the metaphysical plane not to be directly expressed or comprehensible in words, but which dimly perceived by or revealed to Seers and Initiates of old, took the form of certain glyphs or symbols, whereof each nation and race, indeed each man, saw more or less of the meaning according to their Spirituality. The Glyph was there ; its inter-pretation was cosmic and its truth absolute on all planes, but the grossly materialistic man could see only a gross, perchance an anthropomorphic meaning, while the psychic dreamer, perchance in vague intuitive perceptions of the Spiritual meaning, lost sight of the fact that there was a physical and material interpretation or correspondence also true. Such glyphs are, for instance, the doctrine of the Virgin born and all the Symbolism of the Cross, and a moment's consideration shows the reason of all the varying interpretations thereof, each of which is true to the interpreter, save where he denies the truth of other interpretations." As again "when the Christ within is sufficiently developed, a *rapport* with the Christ without can be established exactly in proportion as the professing Christian lives the Christ-life of prayer, self-abnegation, self-restraint, universal love, purity, &c., does he develop the Christ within, and acquire the power of communicating with and assimilating the Christ without, the Master by whom his Initiation proceeds by gradual stages, and there with his powers, according to the Promise, " Greater works than these shall ye do, and nothing shall be impossible for you " (J. W. Brodie-Innes, *The True Church of Christ*, p. 87 and Appendix).

The analogy, the correspondence in fact, is found to be entire betwixt the partial and universal process of Regeneration so called, betwixt the experiences of the individual soul, self-severed and so evolved, and those of the Universal Humanity as represented in the Christian Church by her Incarnate Over-Soul or Lord. The details tally exactly at every station, and the ultimation is the same.

The tradition of Regeneration, as originally taught

by our Lord and His Apostles, finds no place or due allowance made for it in modern thought ; the tide of secular persuasion is dead set against the progress of the New Jerusalem Ark ; but that which *has* been comes again ; the Sacred Vessel cannot drift, but keeps on her Anchorage, below as above, ready to float with her immortal freight by the returning wave.

Those early heraldings of a clear and whole hyper-evolution from this Humanity are yet extant. Eckartshausen, amongst others, assisted to revive them in his day, and Mr. Brodie-Innes has also shown, in continuance, that the Institution of the Christian Church, excellently depicted by him as an actual living organism, is the most remarkable record of any that has been bestowed on the world. The anterior claim and treatment thereof, as a superlative human organism, he indicates accordingly as follows :—

" The cure in the human body is the strengthening of the life-principle, the vitality, till it dominates and subjugates every molecule to the good of the whole body. The cure in the case of the Association is similar, by promoting brotherhood and unity, by subjecting every individual to the life currents animating the Association, by checking us from self-assertiveness, from vainglorious striving after power—in a word, killing the self. In the ideally perfect Church every member bows to the Authority of the Church, and seeks no power or honour for himself apart from his brethren. The Church speaks through and by its priests, but the priests seek neither power nor honour nor wealth for themselves, but are simply the organs of speech whereby the Association communicates with living men" (page 54).

Such an ideal Church, it is concluded, has never yet been realised—any more than any ideally perfect man has ever lived; but if the Perfect Man was manifested, why not *the* Perfect Church? Is not the One implied by the Other as universal Mother, Daughter, Bride, whose Foundation and Head is He? " O mystic marvel ! " (exclaims Clemens Alexandrinus). " The Universal Father is one, and one the Universal Word; and the Holy Spirit is one and the same everywhere, and one is the Virgin Mother; but I love to call her the Church—O amazing birth ! . . . The Word is all to the child, both Father and Mother and Tutor and Nurse. Eat ye my flesh, He says, and drink my blood. Such is the suitable food which the Lord ministers, and nothing is wanting to the children's growth" (*Pedagogus*, lib. i.).

But these things are spoken with reference to the parallel edification and re-investiture of the newly affianced soul by her eternal Antitype which, being otherwise unappropriated in this life, hovers—a free metaphysical entity unconditioned from below— unless, that is to say, the Divine Leader, the kindly light of faith, love and hope—the bare talent—is laid hold of by the natural soul, and brought thereby into identical consciousness, becoming thus psychically conditioned and constituted into a true higher self, so called. The *Augoides* will not be ours until in turn the alien Antitype shall have adoptively gathered back and recapitulated the contents of the chastened selfhood by which it emerged.

Herein the Christian doctrine of regeneration differs essentially from that of re-incarnation, which threatens only upon the neglect of those initials that are wholly present with us, for the edification of an immortal body, that retains the personal relations concrete in their Divine Source.

And if some one already conversant with and believing in such a consummation considers the intervention of the Church as superfluous in respect of it, and that individuals are competent for the attainment of the Union implied, singularly or on their own account, will he not do well to reconsider the *catholic* claim more particularly, and the impotence of individuals even in common life, apart from the society to which they belong? Such are powerless, in fact, to attain their end; the attainment of individual perfection, supposing it possible, is no where and no otherwise valid than by returning as a leaven to promote the Humanity whence it derives.

Aristotle in his Ethics has pointed this out; and his followers of the early and mediæval Churches have shown that the world was in truth created for the sake of the Church, which should be a sublimed epitome thereof and a fitly ultimated measure for the manifestation of its Source.

The two terms of the history of creation or evolution are represented (in the enthusiastic words of the late Anna Kingsford [1]) by two precious and all important dogmas—the immaculate conception and the Assumption of the Blessed Virgin Mary:—

"As the immaculate conception is the foundation of the Mysteries, so is the Assumption their Crown. For the entire object and end of cosmic evolution is precisely the triumph and Apotheosis of the soul. In the mystery presented by this dogma we behold the consummation of the whole scheme of creation : the perpetuation and glorification of the individual Ego. The grave, the material and astral consciousness, cannot retain the immaculate Mother of God. She rises into the Heavens, she assumes (rather is assumed by) Divinity. In her proper person she is taken up, from end to end the mystery of the soul's evolution—the history of humanity and of the Cosmic Drama is contained in the Cultus of the Blessed Virgin Mary."

Now the Schoolmen, from whose lines the above conclusions issue, refer them simply to the Church. They regard therefore no vulgar tabernacle or congregation, no mere aggregate of religious opinion organised into a sect, nothing arbitrary, partial,

[1] See *Biography*, vol. ii. p. 100, by E. Maitland.

indefinite, mean, limited, or irrational. The Church was clearly in the conception of those men nothing less than a sublime synthesis of the whole sub-jacent, representative Humanity; it was a culminant hyper-physical flower and perfection of human life; it was singularly reared by contrition and long culture and finally constituted into an Over-Soul already redeemed, and potent by the tenure of a twofold fundamental and voluntary allegiance for the redemption of Antecedents not yet brought in.

A Church of such calibre, supposing such for the moment, would be constituted upon universal principles—but principles are represented by persons in sacred synods—of perfect parts co-ordinate to one another as truth to truth, bearing witness in number, weight and measure, and form, of every molecule following in strict geometrical order towards the construction of an absolutely free Organism, conscious at every point and polarised to one holy Pattern, as S. Paul exacts.

The Shepherd of Hermas accordingly compares the Church of his affection to a tower or monolith comprising many stones without a single join appearing in the entire compaction, as if it had been entirely hewn out of a rock.

"Hear then," adds he, "why the Tower is built upon the Waters. It is because your life has been and will be saved through water (the contrite psychic element, *i.e.*, to say whether or both individual or universal). For the Tower was founded on the Word of the Almighty and glorious Name, and it is kept together by the invisible power of God" (Chap. IV.).

Yet further, it is shown that the adjustment of such voluntary live contents as are here in question is eminently arduous, if not naturally impossible in any complete degree; and on this difficulty of humanly conforming to the heavenly Patterns, and on the partial overcoming of this difficulty, it has been declared by the greatest of Christian theologians that the arch-history of the Law and the Prophets hangs.

The sacred records bear witness to the obstacles interposing up to David, and from David to the Messianic Advent. But since the Pentecostal Crisis no Church appears to have been formulated in such wise as temporarily even to supply an adequate habitation for the Holy Spirit of God, while many failures are subsequently represented in the Apocalyptic summary passing in review before the Infallible Judge.

What less, in fact, is Bible history than a record of God's dealings with the Elect Hebrew Church in her separative processes and reconciliations, composing as do these a vivid register of experiments divinely instituted and preternaturally enacted, in order to prove, and reprove the adaptability of the human Understanding in collective association with and in proximate relation to its first and final Cause?

Thus, although no such consonant harmony of

intersphered angelic Souls as always is pre-established in the Heavens is anywhere testified as actually realized on earth, the preparations there towards have been abundantly chronicled, and as if, at successive sacramental crises, Resultants had presented themselves in figured forms of personal achievement in process towards an implied perfection not yet attained. "Blocks of Truth," Aquinas calls these, nor are those nobly failing attempts at co-ordination spoken of as altogether vain or fruitless, but are rather held up as salutary forecasts in view of some yet nearer prophetic approach.

Yet more striking examples of psychical approximation towards the Objects of religious worship are indicated by *Shekinahs* bearing angel forms, and of celestial interchangings with the lower spheres, of Theophanies and Monstrances following on sacrificial observances, such as are also spoken of in analogous Holy Books, but of which Christianity presents the only catholic fulfilment according to the judgment of those Fathers and early schoolmen, who, being conversant with every tradition, valued and promoted that of the Incarnation over and above all; for reasons that we can scarcely estimate without entering into the depths of philosophic mysticism.

Scant records are extant of the Essenian Church; the Gospels stand alone without a frame in history, as if to fill up a void, otherwise unaccountable, by the introduction of an Æon that yet abides—a traditional fulfilment of Antecedents that are not of this world's order, consistent with one another nevertheless, and baffling criticisms that are inadequate, as Pilate on the judgment seat, asking "What is Truth?"

"Learners are not encouraged" (says Clemens) "to apply the test of comparisons; nor is the Word given for investigation to be committed to those who have been reared in the art of verbal criticism, and in the power of inflated attempts at proof; whose minds are already preoccupied, and have not been previously emptied. But whoever chooses to be taught of faith is steadfast for the reception of the Divine Words having already acquired Understanding as a power of judging according to Reason. Hence ensues to him abundant persuasion" (*Stromat.*, i.).

Such was the advice followed by the Schoolmen later on during the ninth and tenth centuries, men of the highest intellectual culture and acumen, combined with saintly experience, devotion and erudition, of such degree as is unknown and rarely considered in these days of agnostic endurance.

Augustine, Origen and Clement have severally declared that Christianity contained nothing that was not in pre-Christian systems; it was the same truth more fully exhibited, in other terms, through an unique fulfilment within the precincts, that developed itself all at once in one manifestation. In the words of Gichtel, "A universal Type appeared, giving a picture of the Unity which opened a new Door, and destroyed the Principle of human bondage. The Law of Love was given and commenced operation when the Image of Divine Wisdom was incarnate."

"And why, again, the holy pre-existent spirit was made to dwell in the flesh which He chose, was that His perfection might be made manifest. This flesh, therefore, in which the Holy Spirit dwells, is subject to Him walking religiously and chastely, in no respect (as in the case of the first Eve) defiling the Spirit. Hence, also, it is ordained that this pure flesh, which had been subject to the body without a fault (peccable, but not peccant), might have some place of tabernacle, and that it might not appear that the reward of its servitude had been lost, but have its reward, and the whole creation be justified thereby." For this long errant suffering and highly purified Nature becomes at length, when its term of servitude is over, the Holy City of the Apocalypse, having the glories of both worlds rehearsed within its enclosure for ever more" (see *The Shepherd of Hermas*, chap. i.).

The Church lays down no dogma as to the manner of the Atonement. Gregory Nazienzen, as quoted by Mr. Brodie-Innes, numbers speculation as to the sufferings of Christ "among those things on which it is useful to have correct ideas, but not dangerous to be mistaken"—a quotation which those who affirm boldly what the Church teaches thereon would do well to take to heart. Such matters are left in mercy for faith to feed on, lest none should be admitted to the benefits of Christ's achievement but those who have gone the long way round of following Him in the Regeneration.

The two Catholic Natures, fixed and volatile, Divine and Human, respectively, are implied, one with the other constantly, and their procedure is parallel on the individual as on the universal circuit in each faithful soul, as in the Church that is composed of human beings, set together in various grades, as so many auxiliaries towards the advancement of a total consummation.

And thus the Church which, at her Re-creative crises, by her great high Priests, Prophets and Apostles, being the holy Mother of all holy doctrine, which those in their proper persons severally represent, has been regarded as the only authoritative interpreter thereof, over and above every partial attempt at interpretation, however co-incident be the outcome of any isolated experience or aspect of the One Catholic Truth that has been exhibited from age to age.

Is then the Church a sacerdotal figment? No, not even the fallible outside secular Erastian Church; while she is evermore endeavouring faithfully and laboriously to keep the channels open through the desert of this World. No ritual observance, ordinance, creed or altar need be thought superfluous, if only the fuel be kept ready withal until the time of kindling shall come again. Supposing only, meanwhile, the actuality of such a Pentecostal Church

Catholic and Apostolic as is alleged to have been once existent on this earth at a certain promised crisis of conditional fulfilment,—Will it not be hazardous to disturb her landmarks, to remove either her bulwarks or even the scaffolding of her tradition, until the inner building shall be found complete?

Partial revelations off the line and adverse will be mediately liable to the charge of heresy. The multitude are not prone to philosophy, they need children's food; whereas the progressive soul, evolving by her Principle and in faithful relation therefore to His universal attainment, will have stronger sustenance, though also some schooling, perhaps, to endure at the hands of the old schoolmaster who brings home to Christ.

With all this, and notwithstanding more that might be and has been said for and against the promulgation of Mysticism, it cannot be denied that the differential procedure is inimical to this life, is never completed here, and ought not to be undertaken lightly or of self-will without counting the costs. The "orbicular wound" remains while the Cloud is on the Sanctuary : "Who shall deliver me from the body of this death?"

Very few in any age have been found qualified to bear through the ordeals implied to a successful issue; while it becomes expedient, nevertheless, from time to time, when Scepticism is prevalent and Agnostics rail, to remind some forgetful thinkers of the Everlasting Foundations on which Supernatural Religion rests.

In conclusion, I must add that the latter and greater portion of this final note is transcribed, with permission, from the manuscript of a studious friend, and forms, I think, a fitting and most valuable summing up to my own notes on this very old and ever new subject.

This little work of Eckartshausen was always greatly esteemed by many, and still holds its own, stamping the author as a man who wrote from actual observation and experimental psychical process—of such are the kingdom of heaven.

APPENDIX

THE MARRIAGE OF HEAVEN AND EARTH

Or the Descent of Christ into the Heart
Being a Supplement to
"The Cloud upon the
Sanctuary"

I.

The world will be an alien from happiness until Jesus Christ shall be possessed therein. Then shall felicity reign on earth; peace and prosperity shall abide in all states of life.

II.

Who then is Christ Jesus? He is love, wisdom, power—the source of those pure attractions which generate the light within.

III.

Where He is, there is that dignity of man which blesses the pure and feeling heart; it is He alone Who takes upon Himself that burden by which we are weighed down in the deeps of misery.

IV.

Sorrow and sufferings disappear where His spirit reigns in the heart; we pass in His company days which are those of springtide and hours that are full of delight.

V.

The princes who reign by Him have no peers and love alone is their Kingdom.

VI.

Let us attempt in brief outline a picture of the blessedness which He will confer upon us when the whole of humanity shall dwell in His temple united by the bonds of love.

VII.

The princes shall be fathers of the people, the priests their physicians, and to Him only, the great Saviour of men, shall we owe this beatitude.

VIII.

All who shun one another, all who hate each other, Jew and Gentile, great and small, all who are now in discord, shall dwell together in union.

IX.

Remedies are in store for the sick, whose convalescence is preassured from the beginning; fraternal tenderness watches over the poor man.

X.

There is food for him who is hungry, relief for each who is in trouble; should a stranger arrive, he finds a place of rest and nourishment.

XI.

The widow weeps no more, no longer does the orphan sigh; each is sustained abundantly, for the Lord has care of all.

XII.

The Spirit and the Truth are in the Temple, the altar is served with the heart as well as the lips, and the sacred seal of divinity testifies to the dignity of the priest.

XIII.

Wisdom is the chief jewel of earthly diadems, love rules in the sanctuary, love dwells in the world, love creates its paradise.

XIV.

There is no immolation of brethren on blood-stained scaffolds; we are branches of one trunk and each supports the other.

XV.

Surgeons who now dismember the body capriciously will preserve it wisely as their own.

XVI.

And ah! What do I see? O joy that my heart of flesh will not survive to share! Christian and Jew; Turk and pagan are walking hand in hand.

XVII.

The wolf and lamb are in the meadows; the child is playing with the serpent; all hostile creatures are united by love.

XVIII.

And thou, O wanderer, on the time-long quest, yet a little distance along the mystic road; then shalt thou turn about; little by little already the veil falls from the inner sanctuary.

XIX.

Observe how the flittermouse and screech-owl fly at the rising sun; like error, the night and its prejudices pass into the abode of shadows.

XX.

The new earth begins already; a new age is at hand: the Spirit of Jesus Christ utters: So be it—and it already is.

XXI.

It is there; we say that it is even now in sight; but no—it must rest unseen until the veil falls.

XXII.

Then shall revolution no longer threaten the earth, for He who is the desired of the nations is on the very threshold—He who is Lord is near.

XXIII.

Though myriads of men are butchered in war by the spirit of darkness, he is still doomed to flight, for the victory is predestined to love.

XXIV.

God has recourse to strange weapons when His people forget Him utterly; sin must punish that sin which is the source of evils.

XXV.

This notwithstanding, let a single tear fall from the eyes of the evildoer, and the scene of anguish changes, because his Father is near.

XXVI.

There is One who rules all, One who is leading all according to the ends of wisdom. Many are fighting for Him who do not know it themselves.

XXVII.

Many can conceive of nothing beyond the range of the senses; when the curtain is lifted, what astonishment is in store for the world!

XXVIII.

Then, O arrogant philosophers, you will withdraw in confusion from Him in Whom the wise hope, Who is their light and their happiness!

XXIX.

That reason which you deify is a simple lamp of the senses; he who climbs the ladder of Babel shall not attain truth.

XXX.

Your work shall be destroyed by Him Who scatters the sand at the wind's will: all that is false must disperse before the majesty of faith.